FIRST-TIME MOM MADE SIMPLE

EVERYTHING YOU NEED AND NEED TO KNOW TO
CONFIDENTLY MASTER THE FIRST SIX MONTHS OF
MOTHERHOOD, INCLUDING FEEDING, SLEEPING,
NEWBORN CARE, AND POSTPARTUM RECOVERY

ANDREA MITCHELL

CONTENTS

FREE Baby Milestone Tracker

Keep track of your baby's first steps, first smile,
first words, first teeth, and more.

Moments to Remember
Baby's Milestone Tracker

Milestone	Date	Age
First smile		
First coos		
Raises head during tummy time		
First laugh		
Pushes up with straight arms on tummy		
Rolls from tummy to back		
Rolls from back to tummy		
Grabs a toy		
Gets to sitting independently		
First crawl		
Claps hands together		
First words _____		
Waves bye bye		
First time sleeping through the night		
Pulls to stand		
First steps		
First food		
First tooth		
Says Mama		
Says Dada		
First hug		
First haircut		
First "I Love You"		

Compliments of
FIRST TIME MOM MADE SIMPLE
by Andrea Mitchell

SCAN ME:

INTRODUCTION

Your big day is almost here. Your BIRTH day.

Not the birthday you've been accustomed to celebrating, but the birth of your first child. And if you're anything like me, I'm sure you've been very focused on the pregnancy and preparing for the birth. And rightly so, because your first pregnancy is a profound experience, only to be matched with the joy of caring for your child once they are born.

This is the time to take it all in because you'll only experience your first pregnancy once. If your baby is already born, then I congratulate you on your BIRTH Day. I commend any woman who has sacrificed their body for the gift of giving birth. Having gone through it myself, I give all moms or moms-to-be my full respect. Women are incredible, truly.

And not only do we give birth, but we are amazing at supporting each other, especially when we need it the most. Speaking for myself, my first six months of motherhood would have been extremely different if I didn't have the support of the women around me. And now, I'm here to support you.

Welcome to 'New Mom Made Simple,' a book that can be your beacon of light, your trusted companion, and your source of reliable information from a good friend who has recently walked the same path. I'm here to share my tips, stories, and experiences because I would not have survived without the support of other moms out there.

In other words, think of this book as the ultimate guide to early motherhood, designed to make your journey smoother, less stressful, and, of course, more enjoyable.

Becoming a mother is a profound and life-altering journey that starts the moment you become pregnant. It's a transformative experience that brings with it a wealth of emotions, from joy and excitement to anxiety and uncertainty. As you embark on this journey, it's only natural to feel overwhelmed by the abundance of information, advice, and well-intentioned but often conflicting guidance that comes your way.

Remember, you're already an incredible mother. I mean, think about it: you are carrying a baby for 9 months, which is no small feat. On top, having to deal with nausea and a huge belly that almost forces you to walk around like a penguin is all something worth commending.

And very soon, you will experience the biggest learning curve of your life. Why? Because everything is completely new, and there is a lot that must be learned within a short period. Looking back, I believe that the first 6 months were the hardest without question, and I have no doubt you're holding yourself to a high standard.

My saving grace was having support, information, and resources at my fingertips. "New Mom Made Simple" is here for just that reason—to help you navigate the first 6 months with confidence and give you support when you need it the most.

But here's the beauty of this book: you don't have to read it cover to cover. My goal is to provide you with a well-rounded, user-friendly resource that meets your needs as a new mom. Each section is designed to be engaging and relatable, drawing from real-life experiences to highlight that motherhood isn't always picture-perfect, but it's a journey filled with love and growth.

That being said, I do recommend reading it all the way through and then using it as a resource to address the topics that are important and relevant to you as they come up. *Feeling overwhelmed?* Flip to the chapter on self-care and find strategies to recharge. *Struggling with breastfeeding?* Turn to the comprehensive guide on nursing for practical advice. *Worried about establishing a sleep routine?* I've got you covered in chapter 4, where I talk about awake windows and sleep schedules. The flow of this book is intentional, and there are gems in each chapter, so I encourage you to give the book a complete read.

My own path to motherhood was far from conventional. At the age of 42, I found myself facing the decision to induce labor due to the increased risk of stillbirth after 41 weeks. It wasn't what I had initially planned, and the experience turned out to be one of the most painful moments of my life. However, the birth, despite not going according to plan, was ultimately beautiful. This taught me a crucial lesson: motherhood is full of unexpected twists and turns, and flexibility is key.

Prior to becoming a mom, I battled with infertility for eighteen months, going through a variety of IVF treatments and investigating various paths to having a baby. My journey also included a diagnosis of endometriosis, which was a significant factor in my infertility. After a successful surgery to address this condition, I finally got pregnant.

During the first six months of my son's life, I learned firsthand about the immense challenges and joys of motherhood. The sleepless nights, steep learning curve, and need for constant support were all part of my experience. Fortunately, I had the invaluable support of a mom's group, where we regularly shared our concerns, questions, and experiences. This network of fellow first-time moms was a lifeline, reminding me that I wasn't alone in my struggles.

Throughout my journey, I sought guidance from midwives, doctors, and experts whenever needed. This book is an extension of my commitment to sharing information and support with new moms like you. Of course, you will have questions, and my goal is to provide you with the answers and insights you need. It might be hard at times, but you will get through it.

I also understand that there are multiple places and ways that women choose to give birth. Whether it be in a hospital, at home, or even a water birth, the best choice is whatever feels right for you. Personally, I gave birth in a hospital, so that's the experience I can speak from. I'm familiar with most options since I did research them for myself and can see the benefit in each. But whenever I mention hospitals throughout this book, please apply this knowledge to your birthplace and use the information as it suits you.

Getting to know your body, inside out, and how it works is the first step in having control over it. As you embark on your journey through motherhood, this newfound knowledge will be your greatest ally.

In the chapters to come, you'll start a journey on the first six months of motherhood, exploring the highs, lows, and transformative moments that define this incredible phase of life. So, let's embrace this rollercoaster, otherwise known as motherhood! As a mother myself, I will be accompanying you through every step of this difficult but fulfilling journey!

And once again, congratulations on undertaking this tremendous responsibility; it will all be worth it!

PREPARING FOR THE BIG ARRIVAL

"Making the decision to have a child is momentous. It is to decide forever to have your heart go walking around outside your body."

— ELIZABETH STONE

How much stuff could a teeny tiny baby need, right? *Oh, you have no idea.*

Therefore, I will be delving into the crucial elements of getting ready for your child to make their great entrance into the world. I'll walk you through everything, from designing the ideal nursery to compiling a shopping list that's appropriate for before and after the major arrival.

1.1 SETTING UP THE NURSERY

As a first-time mom, preparing your baby's nursery is an exciting and important task. I will provide you with valuable tips and a checklist to guide you through the process of creating the perfect space for your little one.

For starters, designing a nursery involves finding the right balance between style and functionality. Whether you have a small room or a dedicated space, the nursery must reflect your personal style while also being practical for your baby's needs.

Setting up the nursery is a joyous journey as you eagerly anticipate your baby's arrival. This room will be where your baby sleeps and where you'll spend countless hours feeding and cuddling your precious bundle. It's worth investing your time and effort to ensure the nursery is a special and welcoming place.

Creating Your Dream Nursery: A Step-By-Step Guide

- ***Discover Your Nursery Design Style:*** Begin by identifying your own design style, whether it's classic, modern, rustic, or any other style that resonates with you. Your nursery should reflect your personal taste.
- ***Craft a Nursery Design Mood Board:*** Gather inspiration from various sources, such as magazines, websites, and Pinterest, to create a mood board that captures your preferred colors, styles, and patterns.
- ***Assess Your Nursery Space:*** Consider the size of the room, its shape, natural lighting, and any built-in features. Understanding the physical space is vital for effective planning.

- *Think About Function:* Determine the primary functions of the nursery, such as sleeping, feeding, and diapering. You might also want to include a spare bed should you need to stay in your baby's room.
- *Sketch the Nursery Layout:* Create a layout that optimizes the available space, focusing on essential zones like sleeping, nursing, and diapering. Experiment with furniture arrangements before making any purchases.
- *Select Basic Nursery Furniture:* Choose key nursery furniture items, such as the crib, nursery chair, and nursery dresser. Prioritize comfort and versatility, as these items will be extensively used.
- *Incorporate Nursery Essentials:* Enhance the nursery's comfort, functionality, and safety with essentials like a crib mattress, ottoman, side table, blackout curtains, sound machine, baby monitor, and a humidifier.
- *Integrate Nursery Storage Solutions:* Make the nursery organized and practical by adding storage solutions like baskets, a rolling cart, and a pegboard for diapering essentials.
- *Decorate Nursery Walls:* Add a personal touch to the nursery by decorating the walls with appealing colors, wallpapers, or wall decor.
- *Finalize with Nursery Decor:* Complete the nursery by updating lighting, adding a rug, and incorporating decorative elements to showcase your unique style.

This step-by-step guide will help you create a nursery that not only meets your needs but also radiates warmth and love as you prepare to welcome your little one into the world.

Now, how about some shopping? After all, shopping for your little one is one of the most fun parts of embracing motherhood!

1.2 BABY ESSENTIALS SHOPPING LIST

a. Before Baby Arrives

Nursery Essentials:

- Crib and/or bassinet
- Mattress
- Two fitted sheets
- Two mattress protectors
- Change table (Make sure it's the right height with the top of the table at your waist. Save your back!)
- Change pad
- Two change pad covers
- Nursing chair
- Dresser or shelves for organizing baby's clothes, diapers, and wipes
- Diaper rash cream
- Baby moisturizing cream for dry skin
- Diapers (newborn and size 1)
- Baby wipes
- Thermometer
- Garbage can (I'm a big fan of specialized diaper bins)
- Baby clothing (I enjoyed zippers over snaps)
- Baby socks or full-length onesies
- Muslin wraps
- Clips for muslin wraps
- SleepSack swaddles (such as Halo)
- Breastfeeding tops and bras (if breastfeeding)
- Nipple cream
- Baby milestone blocks for capturing those early moments
- Breastfeeding pillow

Items for Bottle-Feeding (Breast Milk or Formula):

- Bottles and nipples (based on your baby's preference)
- Sterilizer
- Bottlebrush (large for bottles and thin for nipples)
- Formula (if needed)
- Breast milk storage bags
- Bottle drying dish
- Bottle warmer (if needed)

Outside the Nursery:

- Bath thermometer
- Feeding cover (if breastfeeding)
- Breast pump (good to have on hand, even if you don't plan to use it immediately)
- Baby bath (see more in Chapter 7)
- Baby soap/washcloths
- A baby bag with a change mat
- Baby carrier or sling
- Infant car seat (choose one suitable for newborns, either rear-facing or a capsule)
- Stroller with a flat bassinet
- Rear-facing mirror for the car
- Window shade for the car
- Baby-friendly laundry detergent (wash baby's clothes separately at first)
- Blanket for use in the stroller

b. After Baby Arrives

- Baby monitor (if your baby sleeps in another room)
- White noise machine for a peaceful sleep environment
- Knee pad for added comfort during baby's bath time
- Blackout blinds, or shades, are especially useful when implementing sleep training strategies
- Baby bouncer to keep your little one entertained and soothed
- Baby play mat for playtime and tummy time
- Baby nail trimmer (consider using a motorized nail file for infants, transitioning to clippers as they grow)
- Baby hairbrush with soft bristles for gentle grooming
- Baby nose spray for congestion relief
- Fridababy Nose Frida for safe and effective nasal aspiration

1.3 BABY CLOTHING FOR ALL TEMPERATURES

Dressing your precious baby is a joy but can also be a little perplexing. We all want our little ones to be cozy and comfortable, especially when the weather is constantly changing. Did you know babies can't regulate their body temperature until they're about two years old? That's where we come in – to ensure they're not too hot or cold. So, let's learn together how to dress our babies like pros.

Babies are delicate beings with underdeveloped temperature control systems. They rely on the right clothing and accessories to keep them at just the right temperature, no matter the weather. Whether it's a chilly day or a scorching one, you might be wondering how to dress your baby appropriately. Here's a handy tip: always add one more layer to your baby than you're wearing.

They're extra sensitive to temperature changes, and this guideline can be a lifesaver.

Imagine this: a crisp, cool day with temperatures at 65 degrees Fahrenheit or below. To keep your baby snug, start with a long-sleeved onesie and add some pants. Then, a warm sweater or jacket will help keep them cozy. Depending on how chilly it is, toss in a hat, some socks, mittens for those tiny fingers, and a soft blanket.

Now, on those warmer days when the temperature climbs above 65 degrees Fahrenheit, opt for a light, breathable onesie made from materials like cotton or super-soft bamboo. Pair it with shorts or lightweight pants, and don't forget a cute little sun hat. Keep it light; too many layers can make your baby too warm. To determine whether they are comfortable, simply touch the back of their neck—it is the best way to gauge their temperature.

Dressing your baby during the day is your chance to showcase their adorable outfits while ensuring their comfort. Choose clothes that are easy to put on and take off because, let's face it, diaper changes are a frequent occurrence. Be sure to pack spare clothes in your diaper bag, just in case of unexpected messes. It's all about practicality and cuteness.

When it's bedtime, your baby's comfort is paramount. You want them to stay warm but not too warm. The ideal sleeping temperature is between 68 and 72 degrees. So, settle for footie pajamas in breathable materials like cotton or bamboo, allowing their little bodies to breathe. Don't forget a swaddle or sleep sack for that extra snugness. But remember, if your baby is under two years old, it's important to follow safe sleep guidelines and avoid adding extra blankets to their crib.

Oh, and one more tip: your newborn should not wear a hat when they sleep. Just make sure the room temperature is comfortable and they're dressed in their PJs and snuggled up.

As you dress your baby, keep a close eye on their temperature. A gentle touch on their neck or back will give you a good sense of how they're feeling. Adjust their clothing accordingly to keep them content.

If you're using a sleeping bag, use the appropriate TOG for the room temperature. As long as the baby is put to sleep on their back, they are dressed appropriately for the room temperature, not overdressed or underdressed, with their head and face uncovered, you can feel reassured that you are protecting the baby from overheating.

Armed with these insights, you'll soon become a pro at dressing your baby for any weather, and both you and your little one will be ready for the adventures that await.

1.4 AUTHOR'S TIPS: ADDITIONAL BABY ESSENTIALS

- *Basinet on Wheels*: For the first 4 months, I used a bassinet on wheels and then moved him to a crib when we began sleep training. I found the bassinet on wheels helpful in moving him around the apartment during the day and into our room at night. If you have multiple levels, some moms buy two bassinets, one for each floor.
- *Indoor Baby Carrier*: Don't be afraid to have an additional lightweight or cotton baby carrier that you use specifically indoors. This will allow babywearing around the house, not only so you can have hands free but also avoid overheating!

- *Get the BIG BOX*: Stock up on Size 1 diapers. They don't go to waste, and you don't want to run out!
- *Your face is the Best Toy*: Remember that the most exciting toy for your baby right now is your face. Be mindful not to overstimulate them, but I still encourage plenty of funny-face bonding time.
- *Indoor Sleep Tent*: If you're a frequent traveler, I recommend the SlumberPod. This indoor tent covers your crib or playpen and replicates the 'dark room' atmosphere anywhere you go. Especially when you begin sleep training, having your baby sleep in a dark room is crucial. This will make nap times much easier no matter where you are.
- *Sleep Sacks & Swaddles*: I started swaddling with muslin wraps and graduated to Halo Sleep Sacks when my son broke free from the wrap. When he transitioned to sleeping arms-free, I enjoyed Kyte sleep sacks, also known as wearable blankets. Whatever you choose, be sure to buy two so you have a backup should there be any accidents. See more about swaddling in Chapter 3.

And you're all set! You have all the preparations you might need to welcome your little one home. Setting up the nursery was my personal favorite one because it just adds to the excitement!

The next chapter is all about getting ready for your big day and what to expect within the first 48 hours after birth. I'm sure you're feeling a mix of excitement and nerves, but trust me when I say that the best is yet to come!

THE BIG DAY – YOUR 'BIRTH' DAY

"The moment a child is born, the mother is also born. She never existed before. The woman existed, but the mother, never. A mother is something absolutely new."

— *BHAGWAN SHREE RAJNEESH*

We never know how the big day will go, but I want to help you feel as prepared as possible. In this section, we'll look at all aspects of the big day, including packing your hospital bag, coming up with a birth plan, learning about the options for your placenta, and navigating the crucial first 48 hours following birth.

2.1 PREPARE YOUR HOSPITAL BAG

As your due date approaches, it's always a good idea to prepare your hospital bag. Since labor has no set date or time, thanks to this attentive planning, you'll be ready for the special day. I'll give you a thorough list of things you should pack, covering everything from cozy clothing to baby supplies and personal care products. A well-prepared hospital bag can significantly improve your comfort and lower your stress levels while you're in the hospital.

Be sure to check what's available where you're giving birth. The less you need to bring, the better, so check what they supply first and bring the rest.

Comfy Clothes:

- A warm robe or cardigan for added comfort and modesty
- Non-slip socks, slippers, flip flops
- Comfortable clothing for the trip back home
- Nursing bras or easy-to-open bras/tops for breastfeeding

Items for Personal Care:

- Personal toiletries (i.e., toothbrush, toothpaste, deodorant, floss, shampoo, conditioner, body wash, hairbrush, and a face cloth)
- Travel hair dryer
- Lip balm and moisturizer
- Hair ties or a headband to manage your hair
- Essential oils or massage oils
- Sanitary pads or adult diapers for postpartum care
- Comfortable and disposable underwear
- Ear plugs
- Nipple cream
- Breast pads
- Post-partum recovery pants
- Eye mask
- Headphones

Essentials and Documentation:

- Personal identification, insurance information, and hospital registration forms
- Your birth plan
- Cell phone and charger
- A list of emergency contact numbers
- Medications or supplements, if applicable
- Assistance with contractions, such as a TENS machine
- A birthing ball if you plan to use one

Entertainment & Distractions:

- A good book, magazine, or a tablet for entertainment
- Snacks and drinks for you and your partner
- A water bottle with a straw for easy sipping
- Music

Baby Essentials:

- Range of baby clothes (onesies, sleepers, tank tops, t-shirts)
- Hat, socks, booties
- Outfit for the baby to wear back home
- Wraps/Swaddles/Blankets
- Diapers, wipes & diaper bags
- Diaper rash cream
- Pacifier, if you plan on using one
- A car seat

Comfort Stuff:

- A personal pillow or blanket
- A breastfeeding pillow for your baby

- Heat packs
- Soft/Flexible ice packs
- Any items that bring you comfort

For your Support Person:

- Snacks and drinks
- Change of clothes
- Toothbrush and deodorant
- Watch, phone, or timer with a second hand for contractions

Lastly, ensure your rear-facing car seat is installed correctly and you're familiar with how to insert your baby into it. Many organizations offer car seat inspection services; just check what's offered in your area.

As a friendly reminder, you can modify this list based on your requirements and preferences. But most importantly, it is a good idea to pack your bag well in advance, especially in case your baby decides to arrive early. This way, you will feel more at ease knowing you're ready for the big day, whenever that may be.

Up next is preparing your birth plan. Most women don't think of it, but it's an important element to consider before your birth.

2.2 CONSIDER A BIRTH PLAN

The less you need to do or worry about on the big day, the better. Therefore, I highly recommend writing a birth plan prior to the big day. A birth plan is basically a document that states what you would like to happen during your labor, as well as what you'd like to avoid, if possible. It ensures that your healthcare team understands your wishes, and it acts as a valuable communication channel between you and them.

You have the chance to describe various elements of your birthing journey in your birth plan. These specifics may include your preferences for ways to relieve discomfort, the environment in which you'd like to give birth, and any significant requirements. It's a tool for expressing your unique vision and ensuring that others helping you are on the same page as you.

But it's crucial to remember that labor is fundamentally unpredictable, and unforeseen events can happen. Accordingly, an essential component of any birth plan is flexibility. While the plan serves as a guide, it should also acknowledge the unpredictability of childbirth and the necessity for healthcare professionals to help make decisions that are in your and your baby's best interests.

But please remember that it's your birth. I've heard stories of women who felt pressured to make choices they were ultimately not comfortable with, so the key is to make sure you're happy with your decision. If you don't feel informed enough to decide, then ask for an explanation. At the end of the day, it's your decision, and it's important to feel like you're making an informed one. Your friends, family, and professionals are there to support you, not pressure you. It's your body. It's your birth. It's your choice.

The main thing is to create a list of the things you want, such as I want to deliver my baby vaginally and avoid intervention unless necessary, or I would like to have access to a bath.

Two things I was told to request by a birthing specialist were delayed cord clamping and the ability to breastfeed my baby within the first hour.

Delayed cord clamping means avoiding cutting the umbilical cord immediately after birth and waiting approximately one to three minutes. This allows blood to flow from the placenta to your baby after delivery and is said to be beneficial for your newborn.

Breastfeeding within the first hour of delivery allows your baby to get colostrum, the first milk your body produces, which is high in proteins, vitamins, minerals, and antibodies to help support your baby's immune system.

Even moms who plan to bottle-feed exclusively can offer colostrum immediately following birth. However, it is a tricky balance, so I suggest consulting your doctor if you'd like to take this route.

To put it simply, your birth plan is a strategy to guarantee that your birthing experience is in line with your vision by putting your voice and preferences front and center. I'm certainly not a birthing expert, so I signed up for the online course with shebirths.com to feel empowered and prepared for what to expect.

Trust your gut and prioritize you and your baby. Achieving your ideal delivery experience requires being informed, adaptable, and supported by a caring healthcare team. But most importantly, always support yourself.

Author Story - My Birth Day

I was induced at 41 weeks pregnant and had my son at 8:44 pm. My preference was to go into spontaneous labor, meaning naturally on my own, but statistics showed that the risk of stillbirth rose dramatically after 41 weeks of pregnancy at my current age of 42.

All the reading I had done up to that point was about how my body would go into labor naturally because this is what women's bodies were meant to do. Our bodies were built to give birth, and I had to trust that my body knew more about it than I did. Going into labor naturally gives your body time to better prepare and manage the pain.

I had not read anything about being induced and, therefore, didn't take any medication as I was unfamiliar with the repercussions. Childbirth, for me, was the most painful thing I've ever experienced. But in the end, the birth was beautiful and happened exactly as it should.

Every woman's birth story is different, and I think that is where the beauty of it lies. And even if it doesn't go according to plan, as long as mom and baby are happy and healthy, then that's all that matters.

I should have known that my birthing experience would be interesting, considering the journey we experienced to conceive. We tried naturally for a year and a half with no luck. We did 5 rounds of IVF and still no luck. I went to every naturopath, acupuncturist, and specialist to ensure I was doing everything possible.

My last option was to check for endometriosis, which only crossed my radar 2 years after we couldn't conceive. It turns out that at least 4 people in my common circle had it, letting me know it was more common than I thought. The two indicators of endometriosis are typically pain or infertility. In this case, mine was infertility. Yes, I had period pain, but doesn't everyone?

As of today, its existence can only be confirmed with surgery. Turns out, I did have it. So much so that on a scale of 1 to 4, with 4 being the most severe, I was a high 3.

The recovery was intense, but having the procedure was the best thing I ever did because, after the next IVF round, I was pregnant. My first thought was, why didn't I do it sooner? But then I realized that it all works out the way it should. My son and I are two peas in a pod. The timing was perfect, and he is perfect.

As I said, the birth didn't go according to plan, but the result was all that mattered. And I think keeping this frame of mind throughout motherhood is important.

You will be given curveballs every day, and it's just a matter of getting through it as best you can. Just focus on meeting your baby's physical needs and ensuring they are loved, and that's really all they need.

Next up, let's discuss the Placenta! The placenta is a crucial physiological element for your baby during pregnancy, but did you know you can use it post-birth, too? Continue reading to find out more!

2.3 PLACENTA – WHAT TO DO?

The placenta is a remarkable organ that plays a crucial role during pregnancy. It serves as a lifeline, providing oxygen and nutrients to your developing baby while removing waste. Understanding its functions and significance is vital. Some mothers choose to keep their placenta for various reasons, including burial or medical use. We'll explore the options and help you make an informed decision regarding your placenta.

Author's Tip: While considering what to do with your placenta, it's a good idea to discuss your options with your healthcare provider before your due date. This way, you can plan accordingly and ensure your preferences are understood and respected during labor and delivery.

Encapsulate your Placenta

This is where the placenta is dehydrated, ground into a fine powder, and placed into capsules for consumption. This is believed to provide postpartum benefits, such as increased energy and balanced hormones.

Donate to the Hospital

Another option is to let the hospital take care of it. They have a system in place for proper disposal, and you can focus on your precious new arrival without worrying about the details.

Burying Your Placenta

Planting your placenta with a tree symbolizes life and growth. It might seem a bit unconventional, but it creates a unique family story.

Making Jewelry out of your Placenta

Again, this is another unconventional approach but popular enough to easily find companies who create pendants, bracelets, or earrings with your placenta. It is a remarkable keepsake if this suits your tastes and one heck of a conversation starter!

Create Art with your Placenta

Whether it's a simple T-shirt, a placenta print, or even a picture frame made from your placenta, this option is certainly for those who like to get creative and don't mind interacting with blood. Replicating a tree is a popular print, along with wanting to display the size, shape, and appearance of the placenta. Regardless, they're all ways to honor and appreciate this important organ.

Birth Tissue Donation

Donating birth tissue and cord blood can help change lives. It's used for reconstructive procedures to promote healing as well as treat burns and painful wounds for those in need. Be sure to plan for this ahead of time, as it will most likely require special authorization and additional paperwork.

Saving or Donating Cord Blood

Cord blood is the blood left over from the umbilical cord and placenta after the baby is born. It's said to have special stem cells that can treat or cure certain serious diseases, such as cancers, blood disorders, bone marrow failure syndromes, metabolic disorders, and immune disorders. Parents can choose to save their baby's cord in a private bank or donate it to a public bank. Some parents like to save this cord blood with the peace of mind that it's available should their baby or someone in their family need it. Others who are aware of a genetic family condition can certainly benefit from having this at their disposal. That being said, there are no guarantees, so please research the companies thoroughly and make a decision you're comfortable with. On the flip side, donating cord blood allows other families to benefit from these stem cells should they find themselves in need of this treatment.

Hopefully, the list provided a few options to consider for your placenta. If you've decided to discard your placenta, I highly recommend looking at it. It's worth seeing one time in your life, even if you don't plan to keep it.

2.4 THE FIRST 48 HOURS

The moments that immediately follow childbirth are a whirlwind of emotions and adjustments, and they are profoundly significant for both you and your newborn. These first 48 hours are a crucial phase in your journey as a new mom, and paying close attention to the following aspects can make this transition smoother:

Postpartum Recovery Pants:

Consider investing in postpartum recovery pants. These specialized garments offer comfort and crucial support to your abdominal muscles, which have been stretched and strained during pregnancy and childbirth. They can be a game-changer in terms of comfort and recovery.

Breastfeeding or Formula:

As a first-time mom, one of the significant decisions you'll make is whether to breastfeed or formula-feed your baby. Each choice has advantages and disadvantages, and it's essential to understand them to make an informed decision that suits your unique circumstances and preferences. Below, we'll explore the pros and cons of both breastfeeding and formula feeding.

1. Breastfeeding:

Pros:

- **Nutritional Benefits:** Breast milk is often considered the gold standard of infant nutrition. It contains essential nutrients, antibodies, and growth factors that are tailored to your baby's specific needs.

- **Health Benefits:** Breastfeeding provides numerous health benefits for you and your baby. For babies, it reduces the risk of infections, sudden infant death syndrome (SIDS), and certain chronic diseases. For mothers, it can aid in postpartum recovery and reduce the risk of breast and ovarian cancers.
- **Bonding:** Breastfeeding fosters a unique bond between you and your baby. The skin-to-skin contact and the act of nursing create a special emotional connection.
- **Cost-Effective:** Breast milk is free, readily available, and requires no preparation, saving you money compared to formula feeding.
- **Environmental Impact:** Breastfeeding has a lower environmental impact as it doesn't produce plastic waste from bottles and formula containers.

Cons:

- **Lack of Independence:** You are the sole provider of nourishment, which can limit your freedom and independence, as you need to be available for feeding.
- **Potential Discomfort:** Some women experience discomfort or pain during breastfeeding due to issues like engorgement or latch problems. These issues can be resolved with support and proper techniques but may cause initial discomfort.
- **Inability to Measure:** Breastfeeding makes it challenging to monitor how much milk your baby is receiving. Always offer both breasts during each feed to ensure your baby gets as much milk as possible. Your body will produce more milk based on demand.

- **Energy Draining:** Breastfeeding uses a lot of energy; be sure to account for the extra calories and nutrients needed to keep you and your baby healthy.
- **Slows Hormone Rebalancing:** It takes about three to six months for your hormones to return to pre-pregnancy levels. However, breastfeeding can further impact this. As you wean from it, prolactin and oxytocin will drop, potentially leaving you feeling anxious, sad, or irritable. While hormonal change is individualized, a slow approach to weaning is recommended.

2. Formula Feeding:

Pros:

- **Convenience:** Formula feeding offers convenience and flexibility, as others can help with feeding, allowing you to have more independence and freedom.
- **Predictable Schedule:** Formula feeding may provide a more predictable feeding schedule, as formula-fed babies tend to feed less frequently than breastfed babies.
- **Ease of Monitoring:** You can easily monitor how much your baby consumes as formula feeding allows for precise measurement.
- **Reduced Physical Discomfort:** Formula feeding doesn't come with the added physical discomfort that some women experience during breastfeeding.

Cons:

- **Lack of Health Benefits:** While formula provides essential nutrients, it lacks the unique health benefits of breast milk, such as antibodies and growth factors.

- **Cost:** Formula feeding can be expensive over time, as it involves purchasing formula, bottles, and sterilizing equipment.
- **Preparation Time:** Formula feeding requires more time for preparation, including mixing and heating bottles, which can be inconvenient during night-time feedings. Formula can be offered at room temperature to reduce preparation time.
- **Environmental Impact:** Formula feeding generates plastic waste from bottles and containers, contributing to environmental concerns. Various options for glass bottles are now available.
- **Reduced Bonding:** Formula feeding may result in a different bonding experience than breastfeeding, as the closeness and skin-to-skin contact are reduced.

Many mothers choose to combine both methods to find a balance that suits their needs, especially those with low milk supply. As always, remember that there is no one-size-fits-all answer, and your choice should align with what feels best for both you and your baby.

Some moms make the decision ahead of time, while others wait to see if breastfeeding is possible. Some women love breastfeeding and find it very easy, while others don't. Therefore, it is important to consider your and your baby's health, lifestyle, and overall well-being.

The Transition from Colostrum to Mature Milk:

For those looking to breastfeed, here's what you can expect.

Following birth, the first milk your body produces is called colostrum. It's often referred to as 'liquid gold' because of its color but more so because it's high in proteins, vitamins, minerals, and antibodies to help support your baby's immune system. And because it's so nutrient-dense, your baby doesn't need much to receive the benefits.

Around the fourth day post-childbirth, your breasts undergo a significant transition from producing colostrum to transitional breast milk. This is when your breasts will start to feel tender, firm, and full. Your milk supply is ramping up, and your body is adapting to nourish your baby optimally. This is referred to as your milk "coming in." While this transition can be somewhat uncomfortable, it's an entirely natural part of breastfeeding. After about 2 weeks, your body stabilizes and determines the milk supply needed. At this time, your breasts may feel less firm, and your milk will change to mature milk.

Now, let's discuss some other important factors that I've learned to consider post-birth:

Hospital Staff Guidance:

Never hesitate to reach out to the hospital staff for guidance and support. Lactation consultants and nurses are there to provide valuable tips and expert advice to assist you during these initial days of motherhood. They have extensive experience and knowledge about caring for newborns. While you have the time and access to these resources, be sure to take advantage of them.

Breastfeeding Challenges:

It's important to understand that breastfeeding can present challenges initially. One of the most common hurdles has to do with achieving the correct latch. It's entirely normal for your nipples to become irritated during this learning phase. With perseverance and the proper guidance, these challenges often subside, and breastfeeding becomes more comfortable. For me, the nipple soreness subsided after about 2 weeks. So, hang in there!

Swaddling Techniques:

Learning to swaddle your baby is a valuable skill. Proper swaddling can provide your newborn with a sense of security and promote better sleep. Don't hesitate to ask the hospital's nursing staff to demonstrate various swaddling techniques. They can guide you through the process and ensure your baby is snug and safe.

Meal Support:

Nourishing yourself during the early postpartum period is of utmost importance. It's when your body needs extra care and nutrition to recover. Consider arranging for meal assistance from your partner, a family member, or a postpartum meal delivery service. Having well-balanced, easily accessible meals will help you focus on your baby's care and your recovery.

Prioritize Rest:

Prioritizing rest and sleep is vital during the initial days following childbirth. The first few weeks can be incredibly demanding, and you need all the energy you can get. So, take advantage of any opportunity to nap or relax while your baby sleeps.

Establishing a Feeding Routine:

Newborns often need to be fed every 2 to 3 hours, even if they appear to be sleeping peacefully. Establishing a feeding routine is crucial for ensuring your baby receives nutrition to thrive and grow. It's common for your baby to lose weight in the first few days (approximately 7-10%) due to the extra fluid they are born with. Most babies regain this weight in the first 2 weeks but be sure to check with your pediatrician if you're concerned.

Understanding Awake Windows:

Awake windows are essentially how long your baby can handle being awake before becoming overtired. Initially, these windows are incredibly short, like 45 minutes to an hour. This results in newborns having about 5-6 naps per day.

The newborn cycle might look like this: Wake up, feed for 30 minutes, play for 30 minutes, sleep for 1.5 to 2 hours, and repeat. I provide more detail in Chapter 5.

Day and Night Awareness:

It's essential to understand that newborns don't yet distinguish between day and night due to their developing circadian rhythms. This phase of around-the-clock care will gradually pass as they mature. But be prepared for some sleepless nights in the beginning and remember that this is a normal part of newborn care.

Comfortable Breastfeeding Position:

Finding a comfortable breastfeeding position is key to your and your baby's comfort. Experiment with various positions to determine what works best for you. Being relaxed and comfortable can significantly aid milk flow and bonding with your little one. Ask a lactation consultant or nurse to demonstrate a few positions.

Delayed First Bath:

If you've had a vaginal delivery, you may want to consider delaying your baby's first bath. This practice helps maintain the beneficial bacteria from the birth canal, which can be important for your baby's early health. Hospitals typically provide guidance on when to give that first bath.

Umbilical Cord Care:

For most moms, the umbilical cord is cut and clamped after birth, leaving the umbilical stump attached to your baby. With days, the stump will get darker, dry up, and eventually fall off within 1-2 weeks. Do not try to pull it off. Taking care of your baby's umbilical cord stump helps prevent infection. Use only water to keep it clean unless it is exposed to pee or poo, in which case a mild baby cleanser can be used.

Keep the stump dry and exposed to air as much as possible. Fold the diaper below the stump for your baby's comfort and to help with the healing process. See more details in Chapter 7.

Hospital Tests:

Ensure that all necessary tests are conducted before leaving the hospital. These tests may include checks for jaundice and hearing, among others. It's essential to ensure your baby is healthy.

What's Administered at Birth:

Newborns typically receive several things shortly after birth, such as a Vitamin K shot or eyedrops. Check with your doctor to see what assumptive procedures are given so you can confirm whether you would like your baby to receive them or not.

Capture the Moment with a Birth Card Photo:

Creating a lasting memory is important during these early hours with your baby. Take a photo of your newborn alongside a birth card that includes their name, height, weight, and other details. This simple keepsake not only preserves a beautiful moment but is also perfect for sharing with friends and family eager to meet your new arrival.

In these initial 48 hours after giving birth, you're embarking on an extraordinary journey into motherhood. It's entirely normal to have questions and seek guidance. These insights aim to help you navigate this significant time with confidence, knowing that you have the support, knowledge, and resources to make informed decisions for you and your newborn.

Author Story – The First 48 Hours

Holding my baby after giving birth was the most magical experience, and I'll never forget it. Granted, I was so relieved the pain was over, but the feeling of being responsible for this gorgeous little human cannot be explained until you go through it.

I was fortunate enough to give birth at 8:44 pm, which meant that I didn't have to stay awake all night attempting to give birth; I commend any woman who labors for days on end. I also thought how brutal it was to make women go through birth only to follow it up with caring for a newborn who needs round-the-clock atten-tion. This is just another reason to prove how miraculous women truly are.

I was very grateful to have the hospital staff there to help me because I had NO idea what to do next. In my specific hospital, they had a nursery overnight, and anyone who gave birth that day was automatically granted access to the nursery that night. How amazing, right? I couldn't bear the thought of leaving my son with anyone after giving birth, let alone in a bright "hospital" room that felt anything but warm and loving, but the staff highly recom-mended that I put him in the nursery so I could get some rest. Something told me they were right.

I popped him into the nursery and was told they would ring me when he needed to be fed. So, I slept from about 11 pm to 2 am when the phone rang. "Your baby is crying and needs to feed." I went to the nursery, and as I walked in, even though other babies were crying, I could tell which one was my son. At that precious moment, I understood what it felt like to be a mom. There was already a bond established—a bond with my son. It was a beautiful moment, and I was so excited to hold him again.

I brought him back to my room and helped him latch on to my boob. I had no idea if it would work, but fortunately, it did! I was exhausted, but I assumed it was part of the deal. I popped him over to the other boob because that's what I was told to do. And just like that, he fell asleep.

It was a beautiful thing to be able to alleviate his crying and hold him peacefully in my arms while he slept. It felt wonderful. So much so that I didn't want to move him in fear of waking him up. By this time, it was around 2:30 am; I was exhausted but didn't know what to do.

So, I just held him and let him sleep for two hours. I did my best to stay awake; I didn't want to fall asleep in fear of dropping him, but I didn't feel comfortable putting him in the bassinet.

I'll never forget those two hours and can laugh as I reflect on it now. But I remember the feeling like it was yesterday. Everything felt so new to me, and I wondered whether I would ever fall asleep again.

Eventually, I pushed the staff button and asked someone to help me. I felt so silly asking the nurse to come in at 4:30 am with the request to help me swaddle my baby, but I had to throw my shame out the window.

And that was the start of my journey.

Chapter 2 serves as an introduction to your journey as a mother, with essential data and advice for the day of delivery and the initial 48 hours afterward. In this chapter, we learned that by being well-prepared and informed, you can approach childbirth with confidence and embrace the joys and challenges that lie ahead.

Now that the first 48 hours are taken care of, it's time to move on to the first week! Here's to many firsts!

THE FIRST WEEK – WHAT NO ONE TELLS YOU

"The days are long, but the years are short."

— *GRETCHEN RUBIN*

There are innumerable instances of amazement and sensitivity in the first week, as well as restless nights, unexpected feelings, and a sense of being in new terrain. It is a period unlike any other. Now, we will go into the often-overlooked parts of bringing your infant home, which concerns the "Fourth Trimester" concept. We will discuss the inevitable lack of sleep and the changes your body goes through as you start this beautiful adventure.

As much as I wanted to leave the hospital walls and take my little bundle of joy to the comfort of my own home, I was nervous. I took comfort in the hospital, knowing that guidance and support were only a click away. But it was time to take the next step. Here are some things to consider when bringing your baby home.

3.1 BRINGING BABY HOME

Bringing your newborn home from the hospital is a significant milestone for first-time mothers. While there is plenty of advice on what you'll need and how to prepare, it's important to focus on the key items you'll need. Here's a practical checklist for your baby's first day home:

A Safe Car Seat

Hospitals require an approved car seat, both for convenience and legal reasons. You have various options, from infant-only seats to 3-in-1 and convertible seats. However, it is crucial to remember that all infant car seats should be rear-facing for maximum safety. Car seat safety experts recommend rear-facing seating until your child outgrows the height and weight limits, usually beyond their second birthday. Be cautious with used car seats as they can't be reused after an accident, and models may be subject to recalls.

A Secure Sleeping Place

The safest place for your baby to sleep is in your room, not your bed. Whether you choose a crib or a bassinet, ensure it's a safe, non-recalled option, free from soft, fluffy crib bedding and stuffed toys that could pose a risk of suffocation.

Feeding Essentials

For breastfeeding, you won't need a lot of supplies, but nursing bras and a nursing pillow can be helpful. If you're bottle-feeding, you'll need bottles, nipples, and formula, paying attention to expiration dates. You'll also need sterilizing equipment, a bottle brush, and a kettle for sterilizing water. Optional items include a bottle drying rack and a bottle warmer. Bottle warmers can be tricky as it's more work to prepare the milk. If your baby is happy with room-temperature milk, that's usually the preference.

For breastfeeding moms, it's a good idea to have the bottle-feeding equipment ready in case you want to feed your baby breastmilk via a bottle. Regardless of your feeding method, having burp cloths on hand is also a good idea.

Options for sterilizing equipment include a bottle sterilizer machine, microwave sterilizer bags, a microwave steam sterilizer, or the sanitize cycle on your dishwasher. Just remember to only use the dishwasher's top shelf.

Diapering Supplies

Due to variations in your baby's birth weight, it's wise to have both newborn and size 1 diapers on hand. Additionally, stock up on diaper wipes and rash cream for potential diaper rash situations. Ensure your changing table is easily accessible with all your supplies and your diaper bin is within reach.

Assorted Clothing and Sleepsacks

Babies often require multiple outfit changes due to spitting up and diaper mishaps. Try various options for clothing and swaddles/sleepsacks to see what suits both you and your baby.

Medical Care Essentials

To ensure your baby's health, it's essential to consider the following:

- A bulb syringe for mucus suction or the NoseFrida snotsucker
- Baby nail trimmer (electric file) to prevent scratching
- An eye dropper or syringe
- Essential medicines like anti-gas drops and a baby pain reliever (check with your doctor as some are not recommended before six months old)
- A reliable thermometer for monitoring your baby's temperature
- Optional Thermometers: Bath & Room Temperature Thermometer

Bringing your baby home from the hospital is an exciting experience, and you'll soon discover that, initially, your baby needs nothing more than your boundless love and these essential items to begin this beautiful journey.

I always thought that the third trimester was the last leg of pregnancy. Little did I know that there was a fourth trimester! Yup! You heard that right! Here's more:

3.2 UNDERSTANDING THE "FOURTH TRIMESTER"

The fourth trimester spans the three months following your baby's birth. This concept was introduced by Dr. Harvey Karp, a pediatrician who proposed that human babies are born about three months too early.

The idea behind this theory is that, after nine months of development in the womb, babies are not quite mature enough to thrive outside but can't stay in the womb any longer as they'd be too large to deliver. This explains the significant changes your baby undergoes in a relatively short time, evolving from a sleepy, occasionally fussy newborn into a more alert and content 3-month-old baby.

It's also a time of change for new mothers. As your body recovers from pregnancy, you're learning to care for your newborn and adjusting to the profound life changes that come with motherhood.

This transition is so profound that it has a special name called matrescence, coined by Dana Raphael in the 1970s. Defined as becoming a mother, it's the psychological and emotional shift that nothing will ever be the same again, in the most exciting and daunting way possible. What an honor.

What to Expect During the Fourth Trimester

In the initial weeks following childbirth, your body is healing from the demands of pregnancy and childbirth. Hormones fluctuate, organs return to pre-pregnancy positions, and your breast milk flows in. Simultaneously, you may experience postpartum bleeding and deal with the discomfort of a healing perineal area or C-section scar.

While medical consensus holds that physical recovery from childbirth typically occurs within six weeks, your body may not instantly return to its pre-pregnancy state. Keep in mind that it took nine months to grow your baby, so it may take a similar duration for your body to readjust. If you're breastfeeding, your physical transformation might not be complete until you've weaned.

It's common to feel like your body is no longer your own, especially when coupled with the fatigue that comes with caring for a newborn and the emotional ups and downs associated with adjusting to motherhood. Your postpartum experience may not exactly align with your pre-pregnancy expectations, and you might miss aspects of your life before motherhood. It's a lot to process, but remember that you're not alone in your feelings, and it doesn't last forever.

While you undergo significant changes during the first three months after childbirth, your baby experiences a world entirely new to them. After nine months in a warm, watery womb, adapting to life outside can be challenging for your little one.

Therefore, it's recommended that you recreate the environment your baby had in the uterus, especially when they're upset. Imagine your baby transitioning into this big, new world, and it's our job to make it as cozy as possible.

Swaddling is a great way to recreate the sense of safety and security that the womb provides. When they feel safe and cozy, they typically sleep longer, which is always a plus.

Next would be some gentle swaying. Your baby is used to movement from when they were in the womb, and you moved around all day long, so don't be afraid to introduce swaying or rocking when needed. If swaying doesn't work, try some deep bounces. The up-and-down motion seemed to settle my son better. At times, it felt like I was doing an 80s-style workout, but as long as it worked, I was happy!

Babywearing is another great option, whether you're inside or outside. Your baby feels safe being so close to you, and you get to have your hands free—it sounds like a win-win situation!

Shooshing is another trick up our sleeves. That rhythmic 'shh' sound mimics the comforting noises from the womb. Apparently, it was quite loud in the womb, so don't be afraid to shoosh as loud as you need to get the desired outcome.

And then there's the magic of skin-to-skin contact. The warmth of your skin against theirs creates a special bond and a sense of security. I practically lived in comfy cardigans, embracing the kangaroo care approach for that extra closeness.

How to Care for Your Baby

As your baby acclimates to the outside world, they will cry, and that's okay. It's their way of communicating. But if they are crying, they want your help with something.

The best way to figure out what they need is to do the 'checks' so you can start to eliminate what the problem could be. I'll discuss this in more depth later, but it's important to gain a brief understanding for now.

For the most part, they just want a cuddle. Respond quickly to your baby's cries with reassurance, warmth, and affection. This way, they will feel safe and secure and usually calm down more quickly.

My next check would be to determine whether they are hungry. I'd offer a feed again to find out. Next would be the diaper check to see if they were wet or soiled, which thankfully was an easy fix.

Next, do they need to burp or relieve gas? Babies are always upset when they are gassy, so helping them burp or fart is one of the best ways to settle them back to happiness.

Next, I would gauge if they were too hot or too cold. Feel their tummy or back of their neck; it should be warm, not too hot, or too cold. Or just remove or add clothing to see if this helps settle your baby.

It's worth noting that most babies won't fuss if they are too hot, more so if they are too cold. Higher temperatures increase the risk of SIDS in infants 3-12 months old, so be sure to keep your baby's room at the recommended temperature between 68 to 72 degrees.

And lastly, is your baby tired or ready for sleep? I will go into more detail about awake windows so you can have a good feel for when your baby will be ready for sleep, but this can definitely contribute to a cranky baby. Start with the techniques above with swaying, shooshing, skin-to-skin, and even patting the bum or side of the leg to help settle your baby.

Throughout the fourth trimester, your baby will transition from gazing with cloudy eyes to becoming a more engaged and expressive infant who imitates your movements and facial expressions and even flashes smiles. By the three-month mark, your baby will likely be able to lift their head higher during tummy time and begin to push up. As their vision improves and their capacity for interaction grows, their personality will begin to emerge.

Moreover, your baby will develop a more predictable eating routine and a relatively stable sleep schedule by the end of the fourth trimester, offering hope for a better-rested future.

With that being said, I would like to share some tips that helped me navigate this critical and challenging time.

Tips for Navigating the Fourth Trimester

These initial, hazy days won't last forever, but in the meantime, here are some strategies to help you through:

1. Accept That Your Body Needs to Recover

Resting is one of the most important things you can do for yourself. It's critical to recognize that giving birth has significantly altered your physique. You may be caring for a sensitive pelvic area or recovering from surgery. Beyond the physical, processing and adjustment time will be required for your mind and heart. Tell everyone you love about your intention to spend several weeks with your infant, especially your partner. It's important not to feel guilty about focusing solely on yourself and your family. Arrange a comfortable "nest" surrounding your bed, complete with clothing, diapers, water, and snacks for you and your child. Having a partner or postpartum doula in the nest with you might offer many opportunities for relaxation and socialization.

2. Put Nutrition First

While trying to get some rest and taking care of a newborn, eating healthfully is important but frequently forgotten. Make a plan: will friends deliver meals that have already been prepared? Should you prepare meals ahead of time, or should you order takeaway? Consider eating simple, nourishing foods like bone broths, warm, soft dishes, high-protein alternatives, and convenient afternoon snacks. Assume you won't have time for cooking in the first few weeks, even if you and your partner like it. I highly recommend a meal service that's designed specifically to nourish moms during postpartum, at least for the first 40 days. his will ensure you get the best nutrients and care possible while focusing on your little one. Search online for ready-made meals for postpartum moms or get the book called *The First 40 days* by Heng Ou.

3. Prioritize Rest

Don't feel compelled to handle everything by yourself. Prioritize rest during your baby's sleep and ask for support from your partner, family, or friends to ensure you get the rest you need. This is the time to hand off tasks like groceries, laundry, or cleaning to others willing to help.

4. Seek Expert Assistance

When you're at home with a newborn, it's critical to have quick access to expert support, particularly if you're in discomfort or finding it difficult to nurse. Include your pediatrician, midwife/OB, and other healthcare professionals on your list. You may also want to include a breastfeeding consultant, a postpartum physical therapist, a postpartum doula, and assistance with housework, pet care, and sibling care. If you haven't already, consider going to a support group, individually or as a couple, for mental health therapy. Surrounding yourself with other moms or couples going through this stage can be very helpful and supportive.

5. Regulate Expectations of Visitors

It can be difficult for new parents to decide who should visit, when, and for how long. Much like your birthing environment, your postpartum home is a holy area, so who you allow into your new family's world can significantly impact you. Think of two kinds of guests: the ones who are coming to help you and the ones who are primarily interested in seeing the baby. Supportive visitors will gladly assist with household tasks, cook meals, and give you much-needed pauses while holding your infant. On the other hand, guests concerned with the infant may unintentionally cause more stress and tiredness as you may feel the pressure to entertain them. If you accept them, it's a good idea to establish boundaries and be open about your needs.

6. Be Kind to Yourself

It's critical that you treat yourself with kindness. You're undergoing tremendous metamorphosis, and feeling pressured to complete things is normal. Mood swings and weepiness, often referred to as "baby blues," are common in the postpartum period, exacerbated by sleep deprivation. Don't be hard on yourself for experiencing these emotions. However, if you feel persistently sad, excessively anxious, or have thoughts of harming yourself or your baby, it's essential to reach out to your doctor, as it may indicate postpartum depression or anxiety.

7. Prioritize Yourself and Your Baby

Remember, the postpartum period is short; now is the time to rest, enjoy your favorite foods, take quick showers and strolls, and surround yourself with people dedicated to looking after you. Give yourself permission to honestly communicate your feelings to your significant other, a reliable friend, or a caring expert. The postpartum parent needs to be the head of the household and get all the attention and affection they are due.

8. Connect with Other New Moms

You're not alone in this journey. Reach out to other moms for support and shared experiences. Your pediatrician or OB/GYN can recommend support groups, and you can explore local parent Facebook groups and community bulletin boards or meet fellow moms while out and about. Connecting with other moms who understand and are experiencing the same journey can provide invaluable camaraderie and advice, making you feel validated.

The fourth trimester is a unique and transformative time for you and your baby. Embrace the challenges and the joys of this period as you adapt and grow together.

3.3 THE ART OF THE SWADDLE

Swaddling is a traditional practice that involves wrapping a newborn baby snugly in a blanket or cloth. It's a technique many first-time moms find helpful during the initial weeks following childbirth. However, it's important to understand the proper way to swaddle and the considerations for safe swaddling.

Benefits of Swaddling:

- *Improved Sleep:* Swaddling can help infants sleep better by preventing sudden movements that might startle them awake. It creates a cozy, womb-like environment that promotes longer and more restful sleep.
- *Soothing:* Swaddling offers a sense of security and comfort for babies. It can help calm a fussy infant by mimicking the feeling of being held.
- *Temperature Regulation:* A secure swaddle can assist in regulating a baby's body temperature. However, it's crucial not to overheat the baby, so ensure they are dressed appropriately underneath the swaddle.
- *Reduced Startle Reflex:* Swaddling diminishes the Moro reflex, which causes infants to startle. This reduction in the startle reflex helps babies remain calm and sleep more soundly.

Key Points for Safe Swaddling:

- *Allow for Movement:* Leave enough room around the baby's hips for proper hip development. The swaddle should be snug but not excessively tight, and the baby's legs should have room to bend at the hips.
- *Prevent Overheating:* Overheating increases the risk of Sudden Infant Death Syndrome (SIDS). Ensure the baby is dressed lightly underneath the swaddle and maintain a comfortable room temperature. Always check your baby's temperature by feeling their neck or back to ensure they are not too hot.
- *Swaddle Position:* To reduce the risk of Sudden Infant Death Syndrome (SIDS), always place your baby on their back while sleeping. The swaddle should not cover their face.
- *Swaddle Options:* There are plenty of options, but muslin wraps are extremely popular because they are soft, lightweight, and breathable.
- *Age and Mobility:* As your baby grows and becomes more mobile, they may begin rolling over. It's crucial to discontinue swaddling at this point, as it can hinder their ability to roll and may pose a safety risk.
- *Recognize Signs of Discomfort:* Closely monitor your baby when swaddled and be attentive to any signs of discomfort. If your baby seems to be struggling or dislikes being swaddled, it's essential to respect their preferences.
- *Learning to Swaddle:* Swaddling may require some practice to get it just right. Many hospitals and online resources offer demonstrations on how to swaddle effectively. You can also seek guidance from a nurse or a pediatrician.

How to Swaddle:

1 – Lay the muslin wrap in a diamond shape. Fold the top corner down and place your baby's shoulders at the top of the straight section.

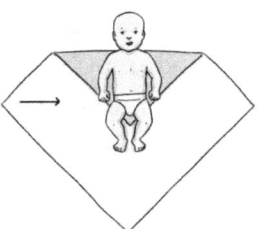

2 – Grab the left corner and pull it across your baby's body. Focus on keeping it snug by the arms but loose around the hips.

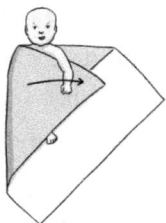

3 – Roll your baby onto their right side and tuck that corner under their body.

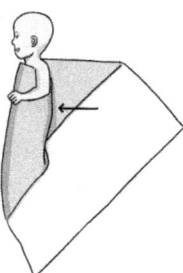

4 –Grab the bottom corner and tuck it into the top flap on either their front or back sides. The top should be snug but loose around your baby's hips and legs so they can move freely.

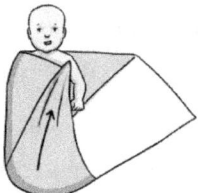 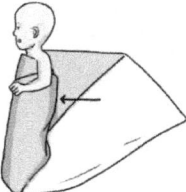

5 – Grab the right corner and pull it across your baby's body.

6 – Tuck the last corner under your baby's body for a snug fit across the arms but loose around the hips and legs.

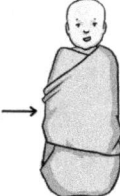

Transitioning Out of Swaddling

It's important to be aware of when it's time to transition your baby out of swaddling. This typically occurs when your baby shows signs of rolling over or begins to break free from the swaddle. At this point, swaddling can become unsafe as it restricts their mobility.

Instead of swaddling, consider using a sleep sack or wearable blanket. These options allow your baby to move their arms and legs freely while providing a blanket's comfort and security. This gradual transition can help maintain a safe sleep environment as your baby continues to grow.

Some moms found it helpful to remove one arm at a time from the swaddle or sleep sack. Do not be afraid to try a few things to see what works for your baby. Be sure to purchase a sleep sack that doesn't curve in towards the chest but rather looks like an upside-down 'V' with straight lines ensuring space around the lungs.

Swaddling can be a helpful practice for first-time moms in the initial weeks following childbirth. It offers several benefits, including improved sleep and comfort for your baby. At the same time, some babies are happy sleeping with their arms out. Trial and error works best to see what your baby prefers.

3.4 SLEEP DEPRIVATION & YOUR BODY

Remember those peaceful nights of uninterrupted eight-hour sleep before becoming a new mom? Well, they're not gone forever, but certainly for the next few months. Thankfully, you're likely to be on a natural high following birth, but it's worth knowing that this will wear off eventually.

Everyone's experience with sleep is different, mainly because all babies are different. I have seen for myself that some babies sleep more than others. It's just the way it is. But it's worth noting that you can get back to decent sleep relatively quickly.

Here's a birds-eye view of my experience with my son:

- In the first few weeks, 3 hours straight was exciting for me.
- At 8 weeks, he was up to 5-6 hours straight sleep.
- At 3 months, he slept 7 hours and 45 min for the first time.
- At 4 months, he woke up 6 times in one night; this was when I started sleep training.
- At 7 months, I felt comfortable that he would sleep from 7 pm to 7 am most nights.
- At 14 months, when he transitioned to 1 nap, he slept from 7 pm to 7 am every night unless he was unwell.

My point is that the first 3 to 4 months will be the hardest, but there is a light at the end of the tunnel.

Understanding Sleep Cycles

Sleep isn't a single state but comprises of two main types: REM sleep (light sleep) and non-REM sleep (deep sleep).

Non-REM sleep includes three stages. Stage one marks a drowsy state, with some awareness. Stage two sees a drop in body temperature, slower heart rate, and breathing, signaling the transition to "falling asleep." Stage three is deep sleep, the most restorative phase.

The sleep cycle, including non-REM and REM stages, repeats four to six times during the night. REM sleep, with rapid eye movements and heightened brain activity, is more concentrated toward morning, while deep, restorative sleep mainly occurs early in the night.

Adult sleep cycles are usually 90 minutes, whereas babies' sleep cycles are about 40-45 minutes, which is why they wake up more often.

Understanding Sleep's Importance

Sleep disruptions affect physical, cognitive, and emotional health. Sleep deprivation robs you of deep and dream sleep, which is crucial for mental clarity. REM sleep helps organize memories and process daily events. Therefore, lack of REM sleep can lead to memory lapses, impacting daily tasks and causing frustration. For babies, REM sleep is important to promote development.

Additional consequences of sleep deprivation include:

- Increased accident risk due to impaired reaction times
- Mood changes, including irritability, emotional fluctuations, and even anxiety and depression
- Reduced immune system function, making you more susceptible to viruses
- Weight gain, as sleep influences hunger-regulating hormones
- Memory problems, as sleep plays a vital role in forming brain connections for memory

Understanding Newborn Sleep

Newborns have shorter sleep cycles with more REM sleep. They wake up easily, thereby experiencing shorter sleep intervals, usually three to four hours at a time, and maintain a light, disorganized sleep pattern.

When your baby is awake, you're on-call to feed and comfort them, waking you up multiple times in an eight-hour period. This type of sleep deprivation can be more demanding than having five consecutive hours of uninterrupted sleep.

Dealing with Newborn Sleep Deprivation

There are several strategies that can help you attain better sleep and reduce the effects of sleep deprivation while caring for your newborn.

- *Sleep when your baby sleeps:* Do not feel compelled to do the laundry or anything else. Prioritize sleep.
- *Acceptance:* Accept that your sleep will be disrupted for a few months, but it's only temporary.
- *Take short naps:* Benefit from brief 20 to 30-minute naps, avoiding grogginess. Nap in the early afternoon, and if your baby's nap schedule is irregular, get help from friends or relatives.
- *Share night-time responsibilities:* Avoid severe sleep deprivation by taking turns on different nights, or if you're nursing, consider pumping breast milk so your partner can take one of the feeding shifts.
- *Encourage self-soothing:* Let babies learn to self-soothe and return to sleep independently, encouraging them to sleep for longer stretches. While they're not fully capable of self-soothing until approximately 4 months, you can introduce the techniques with care.
- *Maintain a healthy lifestyle:* A balanced diet and light physical activity are crucial for sustaining energy levels. Limit caffeine, stay hydrated, and consume fruits, vegetables, and whole grains.

- *Seek help:* If overwhelmed, ask for assistance from relatives or friends for childcare or household tasks. Communicate your needs and utilize available support.
- *Create a sleep-conducive environment:* Avoid heavy meals before bedtime, stressful evening activities, and intense exercise close to bedtime. Limit caffeine intake within six hours of bedtime. Make your bedroom a quiet, dark, and comfortable haven, and establish a bedtime ritual to signal your body it's time to sleep. For your baby, a dark room with white noise is best.

3.5 MUST DO: CREATE A MOM'S GROUP

The amazing moms' group I joined was one of the most helpful resources I discovered as a first-time mother. The fact that every mother in this cohort had given birth within three weeks of one another made it particularly unique. If you happen to run into other mothers due around the same time as you, don't be shy about exchanging contact information and starting a group chat. This connection will quickly turn out to be your lifeline when you are faced with the numerous difficulties of postpartum life.

Knowing that other women in your group are going through the same emotional rollercoaster, having the same sleepless nights, and looking for answers to all the questions that inevitably emerge gives you a great sense of comfort. We had open discussions regarding various subjects, including the use of pacifiers, baby apparel options, and even the finer points like suggested nail trimmers. Nothing was off-limits in those early months of parenthood, and having this loving group by my side made all the difference.

Additional Tips to Navigate the First Week:

- *Preserving Precious Moments*

It's truly remarkable how quickly your child undergoes significant growth in the initial weeks following childbirth. Document these fleeting moments by capturing plenty of photos and videos. In retrospect, you'll be astounded, looking back and thinking, "They were so much smaller back then." While the necessity of these numerous snapshots might not be immediately evident, failing to seize this period means it can never be retrieved.

- *Emphasize Rest, Nutrition, and Baby Care*

During the first week after childbirth, it's crucial to resist over-committing yourself. Focus on the essentials, which include getting adequate rest, consuming nourishing meals, and tending to your newborn. Even when the temptation to venture outdoors on beautiful days is strong, bear in mind that you'll have plenty of opportunities to do so in the future. If you feel up to it, that's great, but if not, be gentle with yourself.

- *Track your Daily Activity*

For mothers who choose to breastfeed, using a dedicated app to monitor feedings can be a helpful strategy. I used a simple one called Baby Tracker. Other moms used Baby+ or Huckleberry. They can all be found on the Apple Store or Google Play Store.

A valuable rule to remember is to begin with one breast, empty it, and then offer the other one. Even if your baby does not consume milk from the second breast, it's a good practice to present it. For example, if you initiated with the right breast and your baby only ingested minimal amounts from the left, commence with the left breast at the next feeding. Continue this pattern. An app can be a valuable tool for keeping track, as it's easy to forget which breast you used last. Encourage your baby to fully drain the breast as the composition of the milk changes from the beginning to the end of the feeding. Moreover, ensuring the breast is emptied can aid in preventing mastitis.

- *Monitor Diapers*

Keeping a record of your baby's diaper output, both wet and soiled, is advisable. This data may prove helpful in the event of illness. Monitoring these aspects can provide you with peace of mind that your baby's bodily systems are functioning as they should.

This is also because your pediatrician may ask how many wet diapers per day or how long you're feeding. Trust me, it's easier to track as it happens.

- *Postpartum Bleeding*

Be prepared for postpartum bleeding, which can persist for two weeks or even longer. It's a wise idea to stock up on sanitary pads in advance to help manage this phase more effectively.

Chapter 3 was all about the first week: From getting your little bundle of joy home from the hospital to caring for your baby and paying attention to your body. After all, if you don't care for yourself and strengthen your postpartum body, who else will? So, give yourself the same love and care your baby gets so both the mother and child are happy and healthy!

Now it's time to move on to the next big thing: feeding your little one! Although I've touched upon breast and bottle feeding already, the next chapter will delve deeper into the basics of feeding.

4

FEEDING YOUR NEWBORN

"If you're a mom, you're a superhero. Period."

— *ROSIE POPE*

A s I write this chapter, I can't help but think back on the unwavering devotion to ensuring my tiny one was adequately nourished.

Feeding your infant is a very special, challenging, and wonderful part of becoming a mother. It's a period of learning, bonding, and occasionally annoyance. In this chapter, I will share personal tales, observations, and helpful tips about feeding your priceless bundle of joy straight from the heart.

If you've skipped to this chapter, I previously discussed the pros and cons of breastfeeding vs. bottle feeding in Chapter 2 during the first 48 hours. I also discuss my recommended feeding schedule in Chapter 5, which coincides with the sleeping schedule.

4.1 FEEDING BASICS

Whether you're breastfeeding or bottle-feeding, here are some helpful tips to make it enjoyable for you and your newborn:

- *Be comfortable:* Feeding can take up to 30 minutes in the early days, so make sure you're comfortable. Make sure your back and arms are supported, your shoulders are down, you're breathing, and you are generally relaxed. This is essentially important for breastfeeding moms as it can affect your milk flow.
- *Listen to your baby:* Your baby might only be a few days old, but they know when they are hungry and full. Be guided by your baby and believe they will tell you what they need. You can expect they will be hungry every 2-3 hours; otherwise, a good cry will be the next indicator. When full, they will close their mouth, pull off the nipple or bottle, turn their head, or possibly push the bottle away.
- *Don't rush it:* Feeding is one of the key parts of the day at this age (and any age, for that matter!) Your baby is getting comfortable with sucking, swallowing, and exploring the feelings of hunger and fullness. Allow you and your baby the time it deserves by staying relaxed and not rushing it. This bonding time is also for you and your baby, so take it all in!
- *Create a Feeding Station:* As I said, you could be sitting there for 30-45 minutes, so you want to have supplies within arm's reach. Most importantly, remember to have a glass of water for yourself. Hydration is key, and this is a great time to guzzle a full glass of water. Keep burp cloths or swaddles nearby and a blanket for yourself to keep cozy. Have your feeding pillow of choice and any other pillows

for a comfortable feeding session. And don't forget your phone to track the feeding and catch up with loved ones.

- *Burp as needed:* My suggestion is to burp halfway through the feeding and then at the end to eliminate any gas. A gassy baby is not a happy baby, so this will ensure the next 1-2 hours are enjoyable for both of you!

- *Feeding on Demand vs. Scheduled:* Feeding on demand means feeding your baby anytime they exhibit hunger cues. In other words, it's paying attention to your baby and not the clock. Feeding on a schedule means feeding your baby according to a schedule every 2, 3, or 4 hours. There are benefits to each, and it's a personal choice. Personally, I did a mix of both in the first few weeks by feeding my baby when I believed he was hungry, but also ensured he was fed every 3 hours, even if that meant waking him up.

- *Feed/Play/Sleep Routine:* When to feed your baby will naturally work itself into a predictable schedule if you follow the feed, play, sleep sequence. It means to feed your baby upon waking when they are most alert, followed by playtime and eventually helping settle them back to sleep.

- *Consider a Dream Feed:* Once your baby's sleep cycles begin to regulate, consider offering a dream feed which is essentially a top-up feed before you turn in for the night. You'll rouse your baby without fully waking them between 10pm and 12am to sneak in the additional feed. The goal is to reduce the chance of night wakings, sync your schedules, and help your baby sleep till a reasonable time in the morning.

4.2 BOTTLE FEEDING AND FORMULA BASICS

Feel free to skip this section if you're breastfeeding but know it's here to refer to if you eventually introduce bottle feeding with breastmilk or formula.

There's a misconception that bottle-feeding lacks the intimacy of breastfeeding, but moms find that closeness in different ways. Feeding your baby, regardless of the method, is a time to connect and relish those small, everyday moments together. And you can still do skin-to-skin!

Finding the right bottle and nipple combination can become a bit of trial and error. It can feel like solving a puzzle, but once you find the perfect fit, it makes a significant difference. Start with a slow flow nipple and make sure the milk fills the nipple to reduce the amount of air the baby swallows. Swallowing some air is inevitable, so burping during and at the end of the feed will hopefully eliminate most gas. Many moms are fans of Dr. Browns anti-colic bottle.

Finding the right nipple is typically easier if your baby is bottle-feeding right from the start since it's all they know. It becomes trickier if you're combining breastfeeding and bottle feeding. Just know that a silicone nipple will never be the same as the real deal, so just find one that your baby's happy with and stick to it.

Cleaning bottles may not be the highlight of parenting, but it's essential because formula and milk can be a breeding ground for bacteria. Everything must be washed in warm, soapy water after each use. Invest in a large bottle brush for the bottle and a smaller brush for the nipple that is used solely for this purpose.

I suggest keeping a small tub of warm, soapy water in your sink and investing in a good bottle sterilizer. Soak all bottle parts in the tub during the day, then clean and rinse everything in the evening; run it through the bottle sterilizer, which only takes a few minutes. The last thing you want to risk is your baby getting sick.

Be sure to discard any unused formula or milk after each feed. You will also need to clean any breast-pumping equipment that comes in contact with your milk.

Formula can be used within 1 hour at room temperature or within 1 day if stored in the refrigerator. Breastmilk can be used within 4 hours at room temperature and within 4 days if stored in the refrigerator.

All women want to know is how much to feed their babies. If it helps, breastfeeding moms never know how much their baby is getting. Moms offer both boobs, and the baby decides how much they want.

A good rule of thumb is to start with 3oz and see how much your baby takes. If they finish the bottle, try to give a bit more next time. Ideally, you want your baby to indicate they are done and have a small amount remaining in the bottle.

This amount will gradually increase as your baby gets older and heavier. Increase to 4oz when your baby is one month old and continue this pattern of increasing 1oz every additional month. But as always, your baby is the best indicator of how much to give.

If you have 6-8 wet diapers per day, their stools are soft, and they're gaining weight, it's a good sign they're getting enough milk.

While you'll feed your baby about 3 to 12 times per day at the start, this will gradually decrease as your baby's awake windows increase and sleep lengthens. By 2 months, you'll be experiencing more like 6 to 8 feeds per day; by 6 months, it will be more like 4 to 6 feeds per day.

The last point to touch on is paced bottle feeding versus responsive bottle feeding. Paced bottle feeding is a method that delivers the flow of milk more slowly, and therefore, the parents are setting the pace. Alternatively, responsive bottle feeding is said to give the baby more control and help them learn to self-regulate their milk intake. Again, I can see the reasoning behind both, and do what feels right for you and your baby. I'm an advocate for believing that your baby knows what they need, so it is best to be led by them.

Formula

Now let's talk formula! Baby formula is an alternative to breast milk, typically made from dried cow's milk powder, vitamins, and minerals. It's mixed with cooled boiled water and fed to babies in a bottle or cup.

The nutrients in the formula support a baby's growth during their first 6 months, after which they can start eating solids. However, regular cow's milk should not be introduced until at least 12 months of age.

Formula is different from breast milk in several ways. Breast milk contains antibodies that help protect babies from illnesses, and its nutritional content changes as the baby grows. On the other hand, formulas maintain a consistent nutritional profile. Breast milk also has less protein than formula, so choosing a formula with lower protein can reduce the risk of childhood obesity.

There are various reasons why a mother might choose to feed her baby formula. Not all women can breastfeed for multiple reasons, such as insufficient milk supply, health conditions, or medications.

Breastfeeding challenges can be daunting, making it unrealistic for some women. Others may choose not to breastfeed or need to return to work. There are also parents, like dads in same-sex relationships, adoptive and foster parents, who do not have the option to breastfeed. Additionally, some women may not breastfeed due to past trauma related to their breasts.

When choosing a baby formula, selecting a nutritionally complete cow's milk or goat's milk-based formula for healthy, full-term infants who are not breastfeeding is important. Price doesn't necessarily reflect quality, so it's wise to check the ratio of formula scoops to water to estimate how long a tin will last. Look for a formula suitable for your baby's age and with a lower protein concentration to reduce the risk of future obesity.

Preparing the formula is a step-by-step process. Always follow the instructions on the formula container and use the provided scoop. Wash and sterilize bottles and equipment before use. Boil water, let it cool to room temperature, and store it in the fridge if needed. Always measure the water first, then mix the formula, shake well, and test the temperature on your wrist before feeding your baby.

Remember that the formula should be prepared fresh for each feed. Avoid storing partially empty bottles of formula, and never warm the formula in a microwave. Instead, use a jug of hot water or a bottle warmer to ensure safe and even heating.

Bottle Feeding Positions

Here are a few positions when bottle-feeding your baby. With any feeding position, ensure your baby is at a 45-degree angle minimum, and their head is above their body.

When ready, rub the nipple back and forth on their top lip, which will get them to open their mouth.

#1 - Cradle your baby

Find a comfortable, seated position with your back supported. Cradle your baby and rest their head in your elbow bend. Sit them up slightly, ensuring their head is above their body. Make sure you're comfortable and relaxed.

2 Sitting position – Baby Facing Out

Find a comfortable, seated position. Place your baby upright in your lap with their back against your stomach and chest, facing away. Tip the bottle so the milk fills the nipple. This position is recommended for babies with reflux.

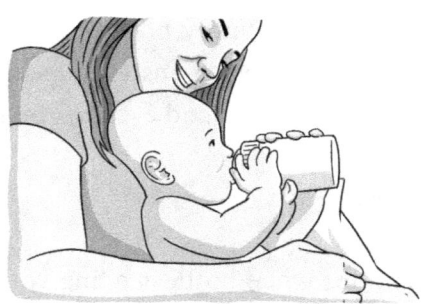

3 Sitting position – Supported Head Hold

Find a comfortable, seated position. Place your baby upright in your lap, facing towards your left or right. If your baby is facing to your right, support their head with your left hand and feed them with your right hand. Keep them close to your body for further support.

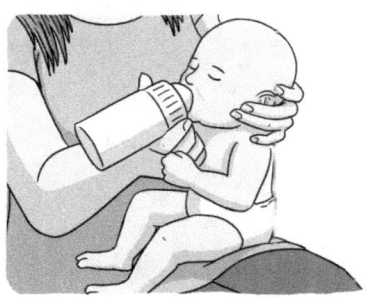

4 - Rest baby on your legs

Sit in a comfortable position and bend your knees. Place your baby's back against your thighs and their head at your knees—this is a great position to interact with your baby and enjoy eye contact.

#5 - Use a feeding pillow

Lay your baby in a c-shaped nursing pillow on a soft surface, ensuring their head is propped up higher than their body—another great position for interaction and eye contact.

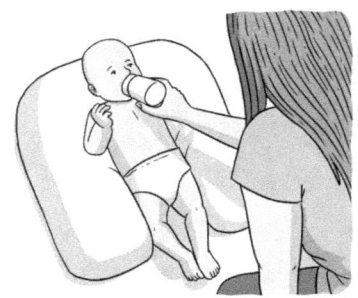

4.3 BREASTFEEDING BASICS

Allow me to share some insights and experiences about breast-feeding. During pregnancy, your breasts undergo remarkable changes in preparation for breastfeeding. Hormones like estrogen, progesterone, and prolactin play crucial roles in this process. As your pregnancy progresses, your breasts will grow, and your areola will darken, signaling that your body is gearing up to produce milk for your little one.

The journey begins as soon as your baby is born. Ideally, aim for that first breastfeeding session within the first hour after birth. This early bonding time can be magical. Even if it's just short, frequent feeds in the beginning will stimulate your milk production.

If you face a cesarean section, don't worry; you can still breastfeed, though it may require a bit more effort during your recovery. Support and proper positioning are essential. In those early days, you might have questions like how often to feed, how long each feed should be, or whether to offer one breast or both. It's entirely normal for your baby to feed briefly but frequently at first. This establishes your milk supply; over time, your baby's needs will communicate with your body to adjust the milk production.

Here, latching is a key skill. A good latch ensures efficient milk removal and prevents nipple soreness. It might take some trial and error, but a proper latch involves taking in the whole nipple and some of the areola. If your baby latches only onto the nipple, don't worry; you can reposition gently.

Breastfeeding positions matter, too. You can experiment with different holds to find what's comfortable for you and your baby. The laid-back and cross-cradle positions can be helpful, but it's wise to try various positions to ensure complete milk drainage.

Breast milk production is all about supply and demand. The more your baby feeds effectively, the more milk you'll produce. In the initial days, you'll mainly produce colostrum, a nutrient-rich, yellowish fluid. This transitions to transitional milk and finally mature milk within the first two weeks.

Mature milk is much thinner and more watery, allowing your baby to stay hydrated. This is why your baby doesn't need water if exclusively breastfed. It is also worth mentioning that if your breasts leak, it is entirely normal.

One common concern is whether your baby is getting enough milk. If your baby latches correctly and nurses every few hours, your body should keep up. Look for signs like steady weight gain, 6-8 wet diapers daily, and regular bowel movements. If in doubt, consult your pediatrician or a certified lactation consultant.

And a friendly reminder: empty the first breast to the best of your ability and then offer the second. Always offer the second breast regardless and start with the second breast on the next feed.

A trick to help you catch up on some much-needed rest is to pump in the early evening, head to bed, and have your partner help with the next feed and awake window. This will give you a decent chunk of continuous sleep and get your baby used to taking a bottle. I introduced the bottle to my son at 9 months, and the bottle refusal was a clear sign that I should have probably introduced it sooner.

Remember, mothers, you're not alone on this journey. With patience and support, you can navigate the world of breastfeeding.

Breast Feeding Positions

Here are a few breastfeeding positions:

1 – Comfortable Recline

Sit in a comfortable reclined position to feel relaxed. Ensure your back and neck are well supported with comfortable pillows or a headrest. Lay your baby across your tummy and bring their head towards one breast, supported by your arms. Alternatively, you can place your baby's head between your breasts and let your baby naturally move towards one breast and start feeding; this is known as baby-led attachment.

2 – Horizontal Hold

Sit upright with good back support. Place a pillow across your lap or elbow on the side you're feeding your baby. Place your baby horizontally and establish a good latch. Then, use the inside of your elbow to support their head and place your forearm behind their shoulders and bottom. With any position, make sure you are comfortable and relaxed. Consider a footstool if needed.

3 – Side Lying

This position is good for c-section moms who want to avoid their babies lying on their wounds. Lie on one side, then lay your baby next to you, facing you. Allow your baby to get a good latch, then support them by placing your forearm behind their back and shoulders.

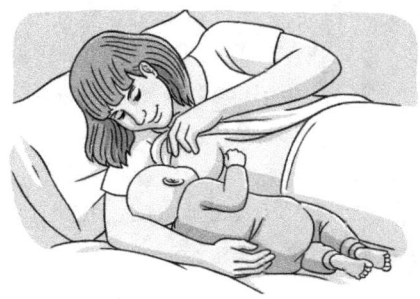

#4 – Football Hold

This is another good position for feeding twins and c-section moms. Hold your baby close to your body and tuck your baby under your arm, like you're holding a football. Allow the baby to latch and use a pillow to support your arm once in position.

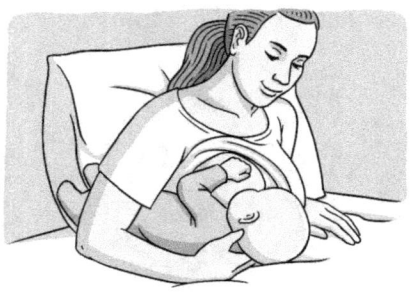

4.4 TROUBLESHOOTING COMMON ISSUES

Feeding your newborn is a beautiful yet challenging journey. Since I have been through it, I would like to share some tips on troubleshooting common issues to help make this experience smoother for you.

- *Cluster Feeding:* This is when your baby wants multiple short feeds over a few hours. It's more common during the late afternoon or early evening. Maybe your baby is stocking up before bed or pumping up your supply, but remember, it's common in these early days. It can be draining, so drink lots of water, respond to your baby's needs, and rest when possible.
- *Latching Problems:* If your baby struggles to latch, don't panic. Try different positions and ensure your baby opens their mouth wide before bringing it to the breast. You can also consult a lactation consultant for expert guidance.

- *Low Milk Supply:* To boost your milk supply, stay hydrated, get plenty of rest, and nurse your baby frequently. Skin-to-skin contact and using a breast pump between feeds can also help stimulate milk production. It's advised not to use a breast pump in the first 2 weeks unless instructed otherwise, as your body determines the milk supply needed for your baby.
- *Sore Nipples:* Sore nipples are a common concern. Using nipple cream and ensuring a proper latch can alleviate discomfort.
- *Engorgement:* Apply warm compresses before feeding and cold compresses after to relieve breast engorgement. Feeding your baby more often and expressing milk by hand can help, too.
- *Fussy Feeding:* Newborns can be picky eaters. Swaddling, a quiet environment, and gentle rocking before a feed can help calm your baby and make the feeding process smoother.
- *Gassiness:* If your baby is gassy, try burping them more frequently during and after feeds. Before they can support their head, sit them in your lap, hold their chin with your index finger and thumb, and gently tap their back to encourage burping.
- *Bottle Refusal:* Some babies may resist bottle-feeding after breastfeeding. Let someone else introduce the bottle and experiment with different bottle nipples to find one your baby prefers. The earlier you can introduce a bottle, the better.
- *Seek Support:* Don't hesitate to seek help from lactation consultants, your pediatrician, or support groups.

Remember that each baby is different, so what worked for me could not work for you. Don't be too hard on yourself and follow your gut. This path has highs and lows, but it's all worthwhile as you see that little one flourish.

4.5 PUMPING BASICS

I want to talk about my own experiences and observations with pumping and preserving breast milk. It's a crucial component of nursing, particularly if you must be away from your child. Here is some information on it:

What Type of Pump Do I Use?

There are plenty of options on the market, but my sister-in-law always told me to get a portable electric pump for the flexibility of moving around. Basically, charge the pump when you're not using it and pump wherever you like. If you're pumping both breasts at the same time, I have found you really can't move much anyway, as you need to hold the cups in place. Next time, I would consider investing in a portable pump that allows the cups to sit directly in your bra, making it completely hands-free. It's said that portable pumps can have lower suction power than traditional pumps, but I didn't have any issue with the suction power.

The Basics of Pumping

Always begin by washing your hands and massaging your breasts. Start with a low suction and then increase it to a comfortable level. You can also compress your breasts softly to extract more milk. Finish by hand expressing into the pump's bottle shield or pumping one breast at a time, depending on what works best for you. Remember, pumping should not be painful. If you encounter issues, don't hesitate to seek assistance.

Milk Flow

Being relaxed is the key to good milk flow. Thinking about your baby, looking at their picture, or listening to their voice can also help you relax and stimulate milk flow.

Breastmilk Storage

After expressing your breastmilk, store it in a plastic or glass bottle with a secure lid or sterile zip-seal storage bags. Label each container with the date and your baby's name. Quickly cool down the milk by refrigerating it or using a cooler with ice packs. You can also freeze it if you won't use it immediately. Store breastmilk in the amounts you typically use for feeding and avoid re-freezing it.

Don't be alarmed by color variations in your stored breastmilk; it can appear blue, yellow, or brown, depending on your diet. Gently tilt the container back and forth to mix. Follow these guidelines for breastmilk storage:

- Room Temperature (up to 77° Fahrenheit / 25° Celcius): 4 hours
- Insulated Cooler Bag with Ice Packs: 24 hours
- Refrigerator: 4 days
- Freezer Section of Fridge: 2 weeks
- Freezer with Separate Door: 6 months
- Deep Freezer: 12 months

Thaw breastmilk overnight in the fridge and use within 24 hours. Never refreeze thawed milk.

Planning Ahead

When you know you'll be away from your baby for a feeding, try to pump at the same time your baby would usually nurse. This keeps your milk supply steady and supports why a portable, hands-free pump can be a great option. If you can't store your milk safely, then discard it.

4.6 RETURNING TO WORK – BUILDING A MILK STASH

One of the biggest questions is how to build a stash of milk when I'm always feeding and wanting to keep my milk flow steady, as extra pumping would create false demand. Building a milk stash is important for moms planning to return to work and wanting to keep their babies nourished with breastmilk. There's a trick to this; however, it takes some planning. Here are my tips:

- *Start 3 weeks before you return to work:* This is the ideal scenario, giving you ample time to build a decent stash of breastmilk. Having any amount of stored breastmilk is beneficial as it will provide you with peace of mind should you not be able to pump one day or forget to bring the expressed breast milk home.
- *Estimate how much your baby needs in one workday:* Pay attention to how much your baby is feeding during your work hours. You'll want to have that much plus a bit extra just in case they are hungry or some milk spills.

- *Introduce the bottle early:* Get your baby used to the bottle around 4-6 weeks of age, with five times per week being optimal for consistency. As they get older, bottle refusal is more likely.
- *Pump three times daily, but only after each feed:* Feed your baby first and pump whatever is left over.
- *Pump at the same time daily:* Your body will start to make more milk due to the increased demand, but it won't shock your system since it's still consistent with your feeding times.
- *Make sure to pump after the morning feed:* It is common for women to produce more milk in the morning, so include this as one of the daily feeds.
- *Aim for 8-12 minutes of pumping:* As it's leftover milk, hopefully, you can get approximately 1-2 oz of milk, but this is a reasonable amount of time to aim for.
- *The goal is to have 3-4 days of stored milk:* This should be plenty of stored milk, assuming you'll be pumping while at work. Plus, this ensures the milk is as fresh as possible. While babies can certainly consume older milk if stored properly, it's recommended to use fresher milk as it will contain antibodies relevant to whatever is going around at the time, such as a virus or the common cold. This is another benefit to breastmilk because it gives your baby constant protection.
- *Continue to pump at work:* When you return to work, try to express milk during the same hours you'd typically feed your baby. It's essential to communicate with your employer about the importance of this schedule. Pumping at work helps maintain your milk supply and keeps you comfortable, allowing you to focus on your tasks.

- *Consider including formula:* If continuing to nourish your baby solely with breastmilk is too much, there is the option to supplement with formula. Your milk supply will decrease, but it will adjust to this new level, allowing you to still offer breastmilk, which is beneficial for your baby even in lesser amounts.
- *Chill fresh milk before combining with other chilled milk:* You can combine milk from separate pumping sessions; just be sure that all milk has been chilled for a few hours, as fresh milk can thaw previously chilled milk. When combining, gently swirl the milk; don't shake vigorously.
- *Freeze pumped milk within 24 hours:* It's important to freeze your milk immediately to preserve the nutrients.
- *Leave room in the storage bag:* Only fill your storage bag to about three-quarters, leaving room at the top as breastmilk expands when it freezes. Also, be sure to squeeze any extra air before sealing. Friendly reminder to date all your storage bags so you can start with the oldest and work your way forward.
- *Avoid Freezer Door Compartments:* Avoid storing your milk in the freezer door as the temperature can fluctuate with each open and close. The back of the freezer is best as the temperature stays the most consistent. Aim for 0° Fahrenheit (-18° Celcius) or colder.

I hope these insights and personal tips make your breastfeeding journey more manageable, especially when you're away from your little one!

4.7 MASTITIS

Let's discuss mastitis, which may not be the most enjoyable aspect of your breastfeeding experience but is something you should always be aware of. Before we start, I'd like to share my experiences and views on what I went through.

Understanding Mastitis

Mastitis is an inflammation of the breast tissue, often caused by a blocked milk duct or bacteria entering the breast. It can be quite painful and may leave you feeling unwell with flu-like symptoms. It's more common than you might think, and I want you to know that you're not alone if you face it. It's most common in women who are breastfeeding within the first 6 weeks of giving birth.

Recognizing the Signs

Mastitis often starts with a painful, tender lump or area in your breast. You might also notice redness, heat, and swelling. Other symptoms can be a fever, chills, or body aches. Your breast might throb or ache, making nursing uncomfortable.

What to Do if You Suspect Mastitis

The first thing to remember is not to panic. I know it can be scary, but it's usually treatable. Here's what you can do:

- **Continue Breastfeeding:** It might sound counterintuitive, but continuing to nurse your baby is one of the best ways to clear the blockage and help with healing.

- **Rest and Hydrate:** This is crucial. Mastitis can indicate that you're overexerting yourself, so rest as much as possible. Drink plenty of water to stay hydrated.
- **Warm Compresses:** Applying warm compresses to the affected breast before nursing can help with milk flow and alleviate some discomfort.
- **Massage:** Gently massage the lump or sore area towards the nipple while nursing to encourage milk flow.
- **Pain Relief:** Over-the-counter pain relievers like ibuprofen can help with the pain and reduce inflammation. Always consult with a healthcare provider before taking any medication while breastfeeding.
- **Empty the Breast:** Make sure your breast is fully emptied during each feed. If your baby doesn't do it, you might need to pump the remaining milk.

When to Seek Medical Help

If you don't notice improvement within 24 hours or if your symptoms worsen, it's essential to consult your healthcare provider. They might prescribe antibiotics to treat the infection.

Preventing Mastitis

While it's not always avoidable, there are things you can do to reduce your risk. Ensure your baby latches correctly to prevent blocked ducts, avoid tight bras or underwire bras that compress the breasts, and change feeding positions. Most importantly, listen to your body. If you start feeling overly exhausted or stressed, take a break.

Mastitis can be challenging, but you can overcome it with the proper care and support. Remember, you're doing an incredible job in your breastfeeding journey, and any challenges along the way are part of the learning process.

Feeding your little one is challenging, but with the right approach, you can get the hang of it in no time. This was precisely what this chapter tackled! From discussing the basics of breastfeeding to making you aware of concerns like mastitis, I made sure to go into every nook and cranny of the world of feeding your newborn.

Now it's time to move ahead and learn more about keeping your baby happy and healthy by settling them in. A healthy baby isn't just a product of its diet, but its sleeping routine! Let's discuss more in the next chapter!

I HOPE YOU'RE ENJOYING MY BOOK.

Please make a difference by leaving a review.

Your gift costs no money and takes less than 60 seconds, but it can change a fellow first-time mom's life forever.

Simply scan the QR code below to leave your review:

Your generosity is appreciated.

Thank you from the bottom of my heart.

5

SLEEPING & SETTLING BASICS

"There's no way to be a perfect mother and million ways to be a good one."

— *JILL CHURCHILL*

As a new mom, it's essential to understand your baby's sleep patterns and help them settle into a peaceful slumber. Believe me, I've been there – those sleepless nights can feel like an eternity, and the quest for well-deserved rest can be painstaking. But don't worry; we're diving into the world of baby sleep together, complete with a few personal stories and insights to make your journey smoother.

In this chapter, we'll explore the intricacies of your baby's sleep patterns, those ever-elusive sleep cycles that dictate your little one's wakeful moments, and their need for rest. I'll even let you in on a secret: the concept of "awake windows" was a game-changer.

It gave me structure and a script to follow when I needed it the most and, most importantly, helped me feel like I was doing the best thing for my baby.

5.1 UNDERSTANDING SLEEP CYCLES

I remember the days when I was a new mom, grappling with sleepless nights and trying to make sense of my baby's sleep schedule. It can be confusing and exhausting, but I promise it gets easier with time and experience. Let me share what I've learned about understanding baby sleep schedules and how awake windows can help.

First off, let me say that every baby is unique. What worked for one mom may not work for you, and that's okay! My little one had his own way of doing things, and yours will, too. But understanding the basics can certainly help.

Newborn Phase

It's true that newborns sleep a lot; we're talking about 14-17 hours per day. This is because they're only awake approximately 45-60 minutes at a time. This also means that you technically can sleep this much as well. The only drawback is that it's interrupted sleep.

If you're waking your newborn to feed every 3 hours, the cycle might look something like this:

- Wake up
- Feed - 30 min
- Playtime – 30 min

- Sleep – 1.5 to 2 hours
- Repeat

The schedule will vary slightly depending on whether you're feeding on a schedule or on demand, which we'll get into more of later, but the point is, you'll be focusing on ensuring your baby gets lots of sleep and is fed as often as they need.

You should start to see longer stints of sleep from about 6 weeks. I chose to let my son sleep as long as possible during the night from 8 weeks old. Meaning, I no longer woke him up to feed after 7 pm. I only fed him if he woke up himself. It's also around this time, 6-8 weeks, that if your baby does wake up at night, they can go back to sleep, usually, with the help of mom.

5.2 AWAKE WINDOWS

Understanding your baby's awake windows is a game-changer. These are the periods when your baby is awake and alert before they become overtired. In the early weeks, these windows are incredibly short – like 45 minutes to an hour. This gradually increases over their first year, reaching 3-4 hours by 12 months. This also results in newborns having about 5-6 naps per day. This quickly cuts back to 3 naps per day, then 2 naps, and eventually 1 nap after they turn 1 year old. Most moms decide when it's best to transition to 1 nap, primarily led by their baby, but as you can see, there is a lot of sleep management in the first year.

I felt that following the age-appropriate awake windows set the best baseline to help structure my day and ensure I was maximizing my baby's sleep.

These were the awake windows that I implemented:

Age	Awake Window
0-2 Months	45-60 min max
2-3 Months	1-1.5 hours max
3-6 Months	1.5 – 2 hours max
6-9 Months	2 - 3 hours max
9-12 Months	3 - 4 hours max

Guidelines for awake windows vary depending on the resource. However, I believe they are similar enough to feel confident that you're on the right track. Trial and error is the best way to determine what's working and what's not. However, this will give you a good framework to start with.

Baby's Sleep Cycles

As mentioned earlier, adult sleep cycles are usually 90 minutes, whereas babies' sleep cycles are about 40-45 minutes, which is why they wake up more often.

This is also good to know because you can easily predict when your baby will potentially wake up and hopefully encourage them to go back to sleep by rocking, shooshing, or swaying either in your arms or the bassinet.

The Importance of Sleep

Why is sleep so important for babies? To name a few reasons:

- Sleep helps keep the immune system happy
- Sleep helps babies grow
- Sleep helps strengthen their memory
- Sleep aids in motor development
- Sleep helps keep their emotions in check

Safe to say, getting proper sleep is something to prioritize for the health and well-being of your baby.

Signs of Sleepiness

Awake windows were the best guide to indicate when it was time for my baby to sleep again, but paying attention to their tired cues was also helpful.

Thankfully, these are easy to identify. These are cues like yawning, fussiness or crying, sucking on their fingers, pulling at their ears, closing their fists, starting to stare into space or a glazed stare, no longer interested in toys, jerky arm or leg movements, frowning or looking upset.

When you see these tired signs, it's time to reduce stimulation and start settling them to sleep. As a new mom, I never thought I would spend so much time trying to get my baby to sleep. The amount of walking around the room, swaying and shooshing was shocking. I recommend capitalizing on the tired signs combined with your knowledge of awake windows and using it to your advantage.

Understanding your baby's sleep schedule and awake windows can be a learning curve, but you'll get the hang of it with time, patience, and a touch of flexibility. And before you know it, you'll become the sleep schedule expert for your little one. Remember, every baby is different, and there's no one-size-fits-all solution. So, hang in there!

5.3 WAYS TO SETTLE YOUR BABY TO SLEEP

I totally get it! The whole world of baby sleep can be overwhelming. With all these buzzwords like self-settling, sleep training, and bad sleep habits being thrown at us, it's easy to feel like we're doing something wrong. But let me assure you, there's nothing wrong with helping your young baby settle to sleep. In fact, it's perfectly normal.

During those early months, typically up until around 3 months of age, how your baby falls asleep doesn't significantly impact their ability to stay asleep. And they're still too young to make major sleep associations. It's after around 4 months that things tend to change.

Once your little one is ready for sleep, you can explore various techniques to help them settle. Let me share some of my favorites:

Swaddling

We already discussed how swaddling is a magical tool for babies under 4-5 months old. It recreates the cozy, confined feeling of the womb and prevents them from startling themselves awake. If you think your baby doesn't like swaddling, it might be because it's not snug enough or they're already overtired or overstimulated. Keep at it, as most babies prefer to be swaddled. But if your baby is consistently unsettled in it, always wanting one arm and sleeping better without, then forgo the swaddling. It's meant to make things easier, not harder. Plus, it's one less transition you'll need to make.

Movement

Babies are used to swaying and jostling gently in the womb, so replicating this motion can work wonders when overtired or fussy. Rocking bassinets, baby hammocks, and baby swings are fantastic for using movement to settle your baby. You can also opt for a baby carrier or stretchy wrap.

Patting/Tapping

When we comfort a baby by patting their back or tapping their bottom, we mimic the heartbeat sensations they experience in the womb. It's comforting and reassuring for them.

White Noise

White noise is a secret weapon for soothing babies. It mimics the whooshing sounds they hear in the womb and can trigger a calming response, especially when overtired or overstimulated. It also masks household noises that might disturb their sleep.

Shushing

Like white noise, shushing mimics those womb sounds. For this to be effective, place your mouth close to your baby's ear and make loud 'shhh' sounds rhythmically.

Sucking

Babies have a strong sucking instinct, so nursing or using a pacifier can be incredibly calming. If you opt for a pacifier, be prepared for some months of pacifier retrieval in the early stages, but it often becomes a source of comfort for them.

If your baby seems impossible to settle, consider adjusting their awake times to ensure they're truly ready for sleep when it's nap or bedtime.

5.4 THE 'TRANSFER' FROM YOUR ARMS TO THE CRIB

I have no doubt you will feel 'nap trapped' at some stage in the first few months. This is essentially when your baby falls asleep on you, and you're trapped in fear of moving and waking them up, especially after working so hard to get them to sleep. Babies know the most comfortable place is in your arms, especially in the fourth trimester. It's warm, it's cozy, and it feels safe. Meanwhile, the crib is cold, hard, and feels disconnected.

And while we love feeling close to our babies, it's not always practical to hold them the entire time as you will need to get a few things done around the house eventually. The moment of transitioning your baby from your arms to the crib can be a memorable one, filled with a mix of anticipation and anxiety. I'd like to share my personal experience and offer guidance for this important step.

Tip 1: If you have an extra hand, you can ask them to place a hot water bottle in the bassinet to warm it up for your baby.

Tip 2: If you can swaddle them before they fall asleep, then they will be nice and snug for the transfer.

Tip 3: Wait at least 20 minutes so you can transfer them when they are in the middle of their sleep cycle and, hopefully, a deeper sleep. Alternatively, transferring them when they are drowsy is beneficial so they can fall asleep and wake up in the same surroundings.

For babies who are already asleep, you will need to reposition yourself so that one hand supports your baby's head and the other is across their bum. As you gently place your sleeping baby in the crib, try to lean over and stay as close as you can until the last second. I always laid my son on his back; however, some moms had success laying their babies on their sides or feet first.

Once supported by the bassinet, remove your hand from under their head and place it on your baby's chest so they feel supported. Once you're able, remove your hand from under their bum and again, place it on their chest or side, whatever works. These loving touches provide warmth and reassurance.

If your baby starts to move and appears to wake, place both hands on their chest and tummy and rock them back and forth while shooshing. The key is to make sure their head rock back and forth, nice, and gently. Ideally, you don't want to have to pick them up and start the process all over, but sometimes it's necessary. You'll get more confident knowing they can be encouraged to go back to sleep while in the crib, so keep at it!

Now comes the delicate part. Once they are back asleep in the crib, slow the rocking down, but keep your hands there. Then, slowly withdraw one hand at a time. Pay close attention to your baby's reaction, as it can vary from one baby to another. Some may stir or wake during this process.

If your baby starts moving or appears uncomfortable, don't worry it's completely normal. I've been through this myself many times. In such moments, simply place your hands back on your baby to offer comfort and security and only reintroduce the rocking if necessary.

If you're placing your baby in the bassinet before they are fully asleep, then simply put them on their back, hands on their chest, and continue the rocking motion with shooshing till they fall asleep. Then slow the rocking down and remove your hands delicately, one after the other.

It's important to know that it's perfectly okay to use physical support during this transition, especially in the beginning. As your baby grows and becomes more accustomed to sleeping in their crib, you'll find that you can gradually reduce the physical support. It's a journey that you and your baby will embark on together, and it becomes easier as you both become more comfortable with the process.

5.5 CREATING A SLEEP SCHEDULE

I'd like to share my experiences and insights on establishing sleep schedules for newborns. As a new mom, I vividly remember the challenges and uncertainties of this endeavor.

It's important to understand that newborns don't adhere to rigid schedules. They operate on their unique timetable, primarily driven by feeding, diaper changes, and the need for comfort. Don't be too hard on yourself or your baby during the early weeks.

Here are some personal tips and advice:

- *Feeding On Demand*

Initially, your baby will require feeding every two to three hours. Trust their cues; they will let you know when they're hungry. Look for signs such as opening their mouth, moving their head from side to side, searching for your breast, moving their hand to their mouth or making sucking noises. Over time, this feeding pattern will become more predictable, allowing you to gradually space out the feeds.

- *Feed/Play/Sleep*

I did my best to follow the Feed/Play/Sleep routine. This means that once your baby wakes, you feed them first, followed by play-time, and then settle them to sleep versus feeding them to sleep. This allows your baby to feed when they are most alert and have a good meal. It's also beneficial for breastfeeding moms because your milk has time to replenish fully, and your baby is getting bigger meals as opposed to snacks.

- *Day and Night*

Newborns often mix up their days and nights, leading to late-night parties. However, you can start to teach your baby the difference between day and night by establishing a routine. Keep night-time feedings calm and quiet. During the day, engage in stimulating activities and let natural light into the room.

- *Napping on the Go*

Newborns love movement because it's like their time in the womb. While it's encouraged to have babies nap in their cribs as often as possible, I highly recommend naps on the go. Sometimes, mama just needs a break! Using a baby carrier or going for a gentle stroller ride can help them nap while allowing you to move about. My favorite trick was taking him for a ride in the car. Either way, I was able to get out and about, and he usually fell asleep within 10 minutes. It's a win-win situation!

- *Bedtime Routines*

While strict schedules may not be practical at this stage, establishing bedtime routines can be beneficial. These routines signal to your baby that it's time to wind down. Consider activities like a warm bath, soothing lullaby, book reading, or cozy cuddle time.

- *Consider a Dream Feed*

As mentioned in Chapter 4, consider offering a dream feed once your baby's sleep schedule starts to regulate. You'll rouse your baby without fully waking them between 10pm and 12am to sneak in the additional feed. The goal is to reduce the chance of night wakings, sync your schedules, and help your baby sleep till a reasonable time in the morning.

- *Flexibility*

Keep in mind that every baby is unique. What worked for my child may not work for yours. Be adaptable and open to trying different approaches. The first few months are about discovering what suits your baby.

- *Remember, You're Not Alone*

It's easy to feel overwhelmed and exhausted as a new mom. But remember, you're not alone on this journey. There's a whole community of moms who have been there and are there now, sharing their wisdom and offering support. Lean on friends, family, and online forums for advice and encouragement.

- *Trust Your Instincts*

While gathering advice and information is essential, trust your maternal instincts. You'll get to know your baby better than anyone else. What works for you and your baby is what matters most.

- *Patience*

There will be nights when your baby won't sleep, and you'll be tempted to scour the internet for sleep advice. Take a deep breath in those moments and remember that this phase is temporary.

Creating a sleep routine for your newborn is an evolving process; there's no one-size-fits-all solution. The key is to tune into your baby's needs, provide comfort and consistency, and trust your instincts.

5.6 SAFE SLEEPING

Ensuring your baby's safety during sleep is paramount. Sleep-related infant deaths, previously known as Sudden Infant Death Syndrome (SIDS) but now referred to as Sudden Unexplained Infant Deaths (SUIDs), are a leading cause of infant mortality between 1 month and 1 year of age. Most of these deaths are preventable, and I want to share some vital practices to help protect your little one.

Follow the ABCs of Safe Sleep:

Alone: Always place your baby in their own sleep space. Bed-sharing increases the risk of SUIDs and other sleep-related deaths.

Back: Babies should be put to sleep on their backs for every nap and bedtime. This position reduces the risk of suffocation.

Crib: Ensure the crib is empty. Remove bumper pads, pillows, blankets, stuffed animals, toys, and even supplies like diapers and wipes from the crib. A safe crib has narrow spindles and sides that do not drop down.

Additional tips for creating a safe sleep environment:

- Your baby should sleep on a firm mattress with a tightly fitted sheet.
- Avoid using soft bedding, comforters, pillows, loose sheets, blankets, sheepskins, toys, positioners, or bumpers in the crib or sleep area.
- If your baby changes positions during sleep, let them be.
- Decorate the nursery as you like but keep your baby's sleep space clutter-free.
- Avoid having your baby sleep on adult beds, couches, or other soft surfaces. They should rest on a firm mattress in their designated sleep space.
- Do not allow your baby to sleep in car seats or swings for long stretches, as they may not maintain open airways. If they fall asleep in these, transfer them to a safe sleep place.
- Room sharing, where your baby sleeps in your room but on a separate, safe surface like a bassinet, crib, or portable play yard, is a recommended alternative to bed sharing.

Breastfeeding can lower the risk of SUIDs. You may breastfeed your baby in bed with you, but ensure they return to their own separate sleep space when you're done. If you accidentally fall asleep while nursing, move your baby back to their bed as soon as you wake up.

By following these practices, you can create a safe and comfortable sleep environment for your baby, reducing the risk of sleep-related infant deaths.

5.7 FROM SWADDLING TO ARMS OUT

It's incredible to watch our little ones grow. Before you know it, they'll walk, talk, and climb the playground. But for now, we face the challenge of transitioning our babies out of the snug swaddle they've been used to since birth.

Swaddling, or wrapping your baby up like a burrito, is all about mimicking the comfort of the womb. It's a lifesaver in the first few months, but eventually, your baby will need to adjust to a new sleep environment. I remember how intimidating this transition was, saying goodbye to the trusty swaddle that kept our sanity intact.

Here are some signs that indicate it might be time to stop swaddling:

Rolling Over: If your baby starts rolling from their back to their tummy, it's time to stop swaddling. This usually happens around 4 months, but it can vary.

Sleep Quality: If your baby's sleep quality is deteriorating, and they're moving around more or trying to suck their thumb, they might need their arms free.

Baby's Development: If your baby is getting stronger and prefers having their arms out, it's a sign.

Settling of Startle Reflex: The startle reflex (Moro Reflex) begins to settle down around 4 months of age.

You'll know when the time is right for your baby. If the transition isn't going well, and your baby isn't rolling over yet, don't hesitate to give it a little more time.

Here's a step-by-step guide to make the transition smoother:

Step 1 - One Arm Out

Begin by having one arm out of the swaddle for 3-5 days. This gradual change helps your baby get used to being unwrapped.

Step 2 - Monitor and Adjust

Keep an eye on how your baby adjusts during the first few days. If things aren't going well, consider swaddling for an extra week or two, especially if the startle reflex hasn't settled.

Step 3 - Both Arms Out

When your baby is comfortable with one arm out, transition to both arms out. You can use a transitional swaddle or baby sleeping bag. If they're not coping with both arms out, you can lightly wrap one arm with a muslin wrap.

The transition from swaddling can be unnerving and it will most likely result in a few sleepless nights. Just remember that it's a step in the right direction, and your baby will get comfortable sleeping with their arms free from now on.

5.8 ROLLING OVER WHEN SLEEPING

I still remember when I walked into my baby's room and saw him face down in the crib. My jaw dropped to the floor, and I rushed over to check on him. Thankfully, he was alive.

The good news is, I was told by my sleep consultant that when they're capable of rolling, trust that they are safe and have the capability to lift their head if need be. This also stresses the importance of tummy time during the day to build up their neck strength.

My fellow moms shared the same healthy dose of concern when they saw their baby sleeping face down. Safe to say, it wasn't our most restful nights staring at the monitor to triple-check they were breathing. My son was close to the 7 month mark when he started rolling in his sleep.

So, here's what you need to know. When babies start rolling, it signifies a growing and exploring baby. The most important thing is to make sure they have their arms free. If they roll over and start crying, you can roll them back over to their back. It's recommended to only do this once or twice, and then just leave your baby to settle on their tummy.

While the first roll from back to tummy is frightening, it can result in a better-sleeping baby, so feel free to get excited about this milestone!

At this stage, the best thing you can do is encourage your baby to roll as much as possible during their playtime. Lay them on a blanket and use the blanket to help roll them over. Do this a couple of times a day so they get stronger and acclimated to the movement.

First off, the excitement. Celebrate those initial rolls; it's a positive sign of your baby's development. But there's a catch: it also means staying vigilant. I discovered firsthand that diaper changes become a bit of a gymnastics routine once they start rolling.

Rolling is an exciting milestone. Cherish these moments but stay alert. Before you know it, they'll be onto the next milestone, and you'll be fondly reminiscing about the rolling days.

5.9 SLEEP TRAINING METHODS

I understand that people have various opinions when it comes to sleep training, but most families who have implemented sleep training have seen the benefits. Let's explore some sleep training basics, from when to start and how to do it with minimal fuss.

What is Sleep Training?

Sleep training isn't just about letting your baby cry it out. It's a process that helps your baby learn to fall asleep independently and self-soothe. It's about helping them use the skills that they already have and giving them indicators to signal that it's time to sleep.

When to Start Sleep Training?

Most babies are developmentally ready for sleep training between 4 and 6 months before they become too attached to specific sleep associations like rocking or nursing.

Can You Sleep Train a Newborn?

Not in the same way you might with older babies. Newborns need frequent feeding and are not ready for long night-time stretches. However, you can establish good sleep habits early by sleeping in their crib as much as possible while providing a dark room and white noise.

How Long Does Sleep Training Take?

The duration of sleep training varies for each baby and caregiver, but most methods take about a week to show results. If you've been trying for two weeks without improvement, it's a good idea to consult your baby's pediatrician.

Is Sleep Training Safe?

Yes, it's safe if your baby is developmentally ready and in a secure sleep environment. Research shows no long-term differences between sleep-trained and non-sleep-trained children. It can also significantly improve a mother's mood.

Sleep Training Methods:

- **Wake-and-Sleep:** Gradually wean your baby off sleep associations like being held or rocked.
- **The Ferber Method:** Like "cry it out," it involves returning at specific intervals to check on your baby without picking them up.
- **The Chair Method:** You sit beside your baby's crib and gradually move further away until you can leave the room.
- **Pick-Up, Put Down:** This method provides physical comfort, like patting or briefly picking up your baby.
- **Cry It Out (CIO):** This method involves not intervening when your baby cries at bedtime.

Sleep Training Tips:

- Establish a consistent bedtime routine from around 6 to 8 weeks old
- Choose the right time to start sleep training, avoiding chaotic periods
- Look for signs of sleepiness
- Put your baby down while they are awake
- Avoid rushing to respond to every whimper
- Create the ideal sleeping environment with a very dark room and white noise
- Be patient and consistent and give your chosen method at least a week to see results

Remember that finding the right sleep training method may require some trial and error. Don't be too hard on yourself if one method doesn't work; feel free to try another or combine techniques. Consistency is the key here.

Author's Story – Sleep Training

I did sleep training for my son at 4 months. The two biggest reasons were 1) he woke 6 times in one night and 2) apparently, I didn't wake up when he was crying for over 20 minutes because I was so sleep-deprived. At that time, I knew it was time to get on board with sleep training because I needed a way forward.

What gave me comfort about sleep training was knowing that he could fall asleep without me helping him and it was a skill that I was helping him develop. Ensuring he wasn't reliant upon me to sleep was the best scenario for both of us. Up to that point, I was happy to assist him with sleep, but now it was time for me to help him develop his own skills.

And while I'd read numerous books on sleep training, I felt I needed proper guidance, so I hired a sleep consultant. It was one of the best decisions and investments I ever made. Not only did it give me a guideline to follow starting at 4 months, but it helped me guide his sleep all the way through to 1.5 years old.

Now, he truly sleeps like a baby.

I'm confident that I'm seeing the benefits of implementing a proven sleep routine early on. I used a company called Sleep Wise Consulting and I highly recommend them.

Here are some benefits of sleep training with a consultant:

- You'll feel confident that you're not harming your baby
- You have someone to contact for unexpected questions
- You can apply your learnings about maximizing sleep as they get older
- Babies can sleep up to 10-12 hours a night
- You won't need to assist them to sleep anymore, saving you significant time and effort
- Establishing optimal sleeping habits that will pay off for years to come

In the first few months, I was happy to 'wing it.' I wanted to bond with my baby and not be too strict about what I was doing to help him sleep. But once his sleep started to take a turn, I knew I needed to upskill myself. After working with my consultant, I felt like I had a 'plan,' it was nice to have expert guidance for areas so crucial to our well-being.

In summary, my sleeping and feeding guidelines were:

- From birth
  - I fed my baby every 3 hours, even if I needed to wake him up to feed (approximately 8 feeds per 24 hours).
  - I was guided by awake windows, knowing that it would be 'round the clock' for the first 3-4 months.
  - Feed, Play, Sleep, Repeat
- From 8 weeks
  - Knowing his weight was normal, I didn't wake him overnight to feed him; this did not affect my breastmilk because he still woke up about 2 times per night anyway, wanting to be fed (About 6-8 feeds per 24 hours).
  - I still fed every 3 hours during the day.
- From 4 months
  - I aimed for a 7 am – 7 pm schedule with 3 naps per day, sometimes 4 if he didn't have long naps. This coincided with 3 feeds during the day after waking and one before bed, a total of 4. If he woke overnight, I would feed and pop him back in the crib.
  - His ideal 3 nap schedule was:
    - 7 am - wake
    - 8 am – nap 1
    - 12:30 pm – nap 2
    - 3:45 pm - nap 3
    - 7 pm – bedtime
  - My goal was 1.5 – 2 hours for nap 1 and 2, 1 – 1.5 hours for nap 3, and approximately 1.75 hours of awake time.

- From 6 months
  - Your baby will most likely show signs that they are ready to transition from 3 naps to 2 naps. These signs include shorter naps or resisting the naps as they need more awake time to get sleepy.
  - Whether it was 3 or 2 naps depended upon how long his naps were and his ability to stretch the awake windows longer.

5.10 FACTORS AFFECTING SLEEP

A few factors can affect your baby's sleep during the first 6 months. A few examples are growth spurts, teething, development, illness, and sleep regressions. This period of growth and development can be somewhat taxing and frustrating for your baby, and their sleep patterns may reflect their efforts. But the good news is, it doesn't last long forever, and there's enough information to make sense of when it's happening.

There's a great resource called The Wonder Weeks, centered on babies making 10 major 'leaps' in development during the first 20 months. The authors want to inform parents that during these leaps, babies will cry more, be fussier, clingy, and cranky, and sleep less. When things seem a bit 'off" with your baby, most likely, they're experiencing a leap. It helps parents understand the changes in their baby's behavior; if nothing else, it's interesting to understand what's happening in their development!

Teething is most likely to happen between 6 months to 1 year, but it can result in unusual nightly wakeups. Illness will also be a factor affecting your baby's short-term sleep. Anytime my baby woke at night, it was important to check on him to gauge what was wrong. But when I couldn't specify the cause, I just said, "growth spurt!"

5.11 SLEEP REGRESSION

Sleep regressions tend to last longer than a few nights of wakeups. When our babies hit the 4-month mark, many may experience a sleep regression, and yes, it's not just in your imagination. It's very much real. The good news is, it's entirely normal, and even better news, it's temporary.

During a sleep regression, your baby's sleep patterns undergo a transformation. They start waking up frequently at night and struggle to fall asleep. Of course, when your baby is awake, so are you.

While most sleep regressions can often be linked to developmental changes in your baby's motor skills and brain development, the 4-month regression has a lot to do with the development of their circadian rhythm. Newborn sleep goes from mainly deep sleep to a combination of deep and light sleep, resulting in more wakeups and wanting help to get back to sleep.

These regressions usually last for about two to four weeks, and while they're common, not every baby experiences them.

Here are some tell-tale signs to help you identify a sleep regression:

- *Fussiness:* Your baby may seem more irritable than usual.
- *Multiple night waking's:* They start waking up several times during the night.
- *Reduced napping:* Your baby's daytime naps may become shorter.
- *Changes in appetite:* They might become less interested in feeding.

The silver lining is that your baby is growing and actively learning about the world around them. They're becoming more engaged with their environment, and this awareness includes you.

Here's how you can manage sleep regressions and ensure you and your baby get well-deserved rest.

Give your baby time to practice during the day

Your baby is eager to master new skills, and sometimes, they might want to practice these skills at night, which can keep them awake. To minimize bedtime practice sessions, provide them with uninterrupted daytime opportunities to practice rolling over or sitting up.

Fully feed your baby during the day

Make sure to feed your baby thoroughly during the day and just before bedtime. This can help prevent hunger from waking them in the middle of the night. At this age, babies can be easily distracted by their surroundings, so try to create a calm feeding environment.

Introduce "drowsy but awake"

Encourage your baby to self-soothe themselves to sleep by offering physical and verbal reassurance as they drift off to sleep. The goal is to help them fall asleep on their own. If your baby is still crying and your soothing isn't helping, you can pick them up or rock them to sleep. It's alright if they're not ready to self-soothe just yet; it takes time.

Make night-time awakenings quick and quiet

If your baby wakes up at night, wait a few minutes before attending to them. They have most likely woken from their sleep cycle and you're allowing them to re-settle back to sleep. If they continue to cry, respond to their needs but keep these night-time awakenings brief and low-key. Avoid engaging in conversation or play, and keep the lights dim. The light from screens can stimulate your baby, so it's best to keep them off.

Stick to your bedtime routine

By 4 months, your baby needs around 10 to 12 hours of night-time sleep and a couple of naps during the day. It's an excellent time to establish a consistent bedtime routine, including activities like a warm bath, changing into sleepwear, reading a bedtime story, or singing a lullaby. Just be consistent with your approach. If your baby sleeps longer than usual in the morning, it's alright to wake them up at the same time each day.

Keep the room dark

Maintain a dark environment when putting your baby down for a nap to promote better sleep. Darkness can help them fall back asleep if they wake up too early. In the morning, ensure natural sunlight fills the room as it helps regulate the sleep-wake cycle.

Pay attention to sleep cues

Yawning, eye rubbing, fussiness, and a lack of interest are classic signs of a tired baby. When you notice these cues, try to get your baby to a quiet space to rest. Promptly responding to these signals can mean the difference between helping them fall asleep or dealing with an overtired, sleep-resistant baby.

Stick with your soothing practices

It's perfectly fine to nurse your baby to sleep or rock them to slumber during this challenging time. While these tactics will need to be phased out to ensure your baby isn't reliant on you to fall sleep, they offer comfort to your baby at the moment. Other soothing techniques like gentle shushing or offering a pacifier can also be helpful.

Adapt to your baby's needs

Babies may doze off in various places during the day, like the swing, the car, the stroller, or the bassinet. However, what works for them one day may not work the next. Be open to trying different soothing methods to find what works best for your baby.

Shower your baby with love and affection

Hugs, cuddles, and kisses can provide comfort and make your baby feel cherished. It's also a meaningful way to bond as they grow and develop.

Remember that sleep regressions are a phase, and they won't last forever. Try to get as much sleep as you can during this time and maintain consistency in your approach.

5.12 AUTHOR'S TIPS: GOOD THINGS TO KNOW

As it concerns sleep, here are a few additional things you can expect during the first 6 months:

- You will see drastic changes in your baby's sleep times. For example, they will go from sleeping 2-3 hours during the day to 45 minutes. It's normal as they become more aware, and their brain develops; just go with it and stick to your routine!
- From about 3 months, try to limit any day's sleep to 3 hours max.
- Babies can be quite noisy when they sleep; just to give you a heads up that it's normal!
- The last nap of the day will be the hardest for them to fall asleep independently, so feel free to assist them by rocking or swaying for this one. I would take him for a walk in a lay-flat stroller so I could get some fresh air simultaneously.

So, to all you first-time moms, embrace the sleep mission. It's not just about getting your baby to sleep; it's about claiming back a slice of your sanity, and, believe me, a more rested you is a better you.

So, chapter five focused on one of the most challenging aspects of motherhood: sleeping! From understanding sleep cycles to creating a sleep schedule for your babies, I gave you all the tips and tricks I've learned as a mother myself!

Moving on, the next chapter will dive into what a baby is associated with the most: crying! Of course, occasional crying is normal for your little one, but what if there's an underlying reason? Let's find out in the next chapter!

6

NAVIGATING BABY TEARS

"Being a mom has made me so tired. And so happy."

— *TINA FEY*

Being a mother is a unique experience full of happy and loving moments and, of course, anxious ones. At some point, all mothers have struggled to figure out why their baby cries and how to give them the most comfort and care. With love, confidence, and the remarkable intuition that comes with being a mother, you can meet your child's needs.

6.1 THE CRYING CHECKLIST

I understand that deciphering your baby's cries and knowing how to respond can be quite a puzzle. Crying is their primary means of communication, and being attentive is crucial. Here's a checklist to help you figure out what might be causing your baby's distress:

- *Hunger or Thirst:* Babies often need to be fed frequently. Even if they've recently eaten, try offering more to see if it eases their crying.
- *Diaper Check:* Sometimes, discomfort may stem from a wet or dirty diaper. So, ensure it's clean and dry.
- *Temperature:* Make sure your baby is dressed appropriately for the weather or room temperature. Ensure their clothes are comfortable and not too tight.
- *Fatigue:* If your baby has been awake for an extended period, try swaddling, rocking, or patting to help them settle and sleep.
- *Gas or Wind:* Gently holding your baby upright and patting their back can help alleviate discomfort.
- *Emotional Needs:* Infants need plenty of close contact and reassurance. So, it is no surprise that a comforting cuddle can work wonders.
- *Sleep Environment:* Some babies prefer quiet, dark rooms, while others find comfort in noisy, well-lit spaces. Find what suits your little one.
- *Health Concerns:* If your baby's crying differs from their usual pattern, or if you suspect illness, consult your pediatrician.

If all else fails, I would keep a bottle of baby pain reliever handy, which came to the rescue with just one dose. Remember that every baby is unique, and what works for one may not work for another. Using this checklist can help you better understand and respond to your baby's cries, ensuring they receive the comfort and care they need.

6.2 A GASSY BABY IS AN UNHAPPY BABY

You've probably observed that infants may make a lot of noise, with gas frequently taking center stage in their orchestra of noises. Let's examine the causes of baby gas and discuss why it's such a frequent occurrence.

First, it's essential to understand that everyone, including babies, produces and releases gas. As food travels through the digestive system, the small intestine absorbs nutrients while the large intestine processes the leftovers, generating gas. Burping releases some gas from the stomach, but the rest reaches the rectum, typically expelled through bowel movements or flatulence.

For newborns, gas is even more prevalent due to their immature digestive systems. They produce a lot of gas, often exacerbated by the air they swallow while feeding or crying. While it's common for babies to be gassy, the frequency of gas is generally not a cause for concern. Babies might appear uncomfortable and fussy when they have gas that needs to be released, but it's unusual for them to experience actual pain due to gas.

If you suspect your baby is uncomfortable, especially if they squirm and pull up their legs, they may have trapped gas. Confirm this by trying gas-relief techniques like burping or changing their position. If your baby seems better after passing gas, it's a clear sign that gas was causing their discomfort.

Now, let's discuss a few ways to help your gassy newborn find relief:

- Place your baby on a flat surface, back down, and gently massage their belly in a clockwise motion.
- Lay them on their back, grab both feet, and bend their knees up to their chest like a squat.

- If bending both feet at the same time doesn't work, try one leg at a time in a bicycle motion.
- Place the baby over your leg, face down, so your leg puts pressure on their tummy.
- Consider giving your baby a warm bath to alleviate discomfort.
- Consult your pediatrician if you need to explore gas drops, formula changes, or diet modifications.

Lastly, here are some methods to prevent excess gas in your baby:

- Ensure thorough burping during and after feedings to minimize air intake.
- Adjust the flow rate during feeding, whether breastfeeding or bottle-feeding, to control air ingestion.
- Check your baby's latch if breastfeeding to ensure proper attachment and minimize air swallowing.
- Tilt the bottle at an angle that fills the entire nipple with milk during bottle feeding to reduce air intake.
- Ensure your baby's head is elevated during feeding to help gas rise to the top of their stomach.
- Examine your diet if you breastfeed, as certain foods can cause gas in both you and your baby.

With a bit of knowledge and some techniques, you and your baby will navigate this phase just fine!

6.3 COLIC AND CRYING

I understand how overwhelming it can be when your baby is crying incessantly, possibly experiencing colic. My heart goes out to each of you, as I've been through the same challenging

NAVIGATING BABY TEARS | 131

moments. Here's some information and personal insights to help you navigate this trying time:

Colic, often characterized by crying for more than 3 hours a day, is not uncommon. Approximately one in five babies go through this phase, typically starting around 3 weeks of age, peaking between 4 and 6 weeks, and often improving by the time they're 12 weeks old.

Colic is also identified by an intense cough, often referred to as a 'seal bark.' During these episodes, your little one may be in discomfort, clenching their fists, curling their legs, and having a swollen belly. The crying can last for varying durations, but it often eases when the baby is tired or has passed gas or stool.

The causes of colic can be quite elusive, but factors like gas, hunger, overfeeding, or emotional states like fear or frustration might contribute. While the exact cause is often unknown, it will eventually subside.

Your baby's healthcare provider can diagnose colic by discussing your baby's history and symptoms and performing an examination to rule out other medical issues.

It's important to note that if you're breastfeeding, some foods you consume may trigger colic. Avoiding caffeine, chocolate, dairy products, and nuts for a few weeks could make a difference. Additionally, check if the medicines you're taking or the formula you're bottle-feeding are contributing to the issue.

As for comforting your little one, it can be a bit of trial and error, as every baby is unique. Here are some methods that might help:

- Allow your baby to finish nursing on one breast before offering the other, ensuring they get the soothing hindmilk.

- Swaddle your baby tightly in a blanket.
- Hold and cuddle your baby, or use an infant carrier for closeness.
- Gently rock your baby to calm them and help with gas.
- Sing to your baby, as your voice can be comforting.
- Place your baby in an upright position to aid with gas and heartburn.
- Consider using a warm towel or water bottle on your baby's tummy.
- Remember to lay your baby on their stomach when awake, but never let them sleep in that position.
- Offer a pacifier to help soothe your baby.
- Going for a walk in a stroller or a drive in a car seat can sometimes work wonders.
- Create white noise with a fan, vacuum cleaner, or other devices.

The good news is that colic tends to resolve on its own by 3 to 4 months of age, and there are usually no long-term complications to worry about.

I hope these tips provide some comfort and guidance as you navigate this challenging phase with your little one. Hang in there!

6.4 TEETHING

Teething, a significant milestone in your baby's development, can cause irritability, crying, and night wakeups as the teeth reach the gums' surface. Teething typically begins between 4 and 7 months of age. However, it's perfectly normal if your little one decides to start a bit earlier or later. Teething symptoms often precede the actual appearance of the tooth. Look out for these signs:

- *Excessive drooling:* Your baby may become a tiny waterfall.
- *Chewing tendencies:* They'll gnaw on hard objects to alleviate the discomfort as pressure provides relief.
- *Swollen and tender gums:* Your baby's gums may become red and swollen. Offer refrigerated teething toys for additional relief.
- *Mild irritability, crying, or a low-grade fever:* Your baby might become fussier, and a slight increase in temperature is possible.

It's essential to note that teething should not lead to vomiting, diarrhea, inconsolable crying, or a temperature above 100.4 degrees Fahrenheit. If any of these severe symptoms occur, contact your pediatrician immediately. It's crucial to differentiate between teething-related discomfort and potential medical issues.

Now, how can you best support your baby during teething? Here are some straightforward steps:

- *Gentle gum massage:* Use a clean finger to gently massage your baby's sore gums, which can provide relief.
- *Teething rings:* Search for teething rings made of firm rubber, as they can offer relief, especially when slightly chilled. Avoid freezing them, as it can be more painful than helpful.

Consult your pediatrician if these methods don't alleviate your baby's discomfort. They can provide guidance on using over-the-counter pain relievers, considering your baby's age and health history.

Avoid using gels that you rub on your baby's gums, as teething babies drool a lot, and the drool can wash away the medication. Additionally, these gels can numb the back of your baby's throat, interfering with their ability to swallow, which isn't safe.

Lastly, it's crucial to steer clear of teething tablets, as certain products have raised safety concerns due to their unregulated belladonna/deadly nightshade content.

Patience and proper care will help you and your little one navigate this phase successfully!

Next up, we'll be looking at the overall well-being of your little one by discussing issues that your baby may face, risking its health. So, keep reading!

7

BABY'S HEALTH AND WELL-BEING

"A baby is something you carry inside you for nine months, in your arms for three years, and in your heart till the day you die."

— *MARY MASON*

The experience of being a mother for the first time has been nothing short of amazing. In this chapter, we'll explore the vital areas of your baby's health and well-being, and I'll share the experiences and knowledge I've learned along the road.

7.1 SIGNS OF ILLNESS

For starters, let's talk about closely monitoring your precious newborn's health. Little ones are more susceptible to infections, especially in their first month, so it's important to be vigilant, particularly in the initial 7 days.

Feeding is a crucial indicator of a healthy newborn. They should be enthusiastic eaters, so if your baby isn't feeding well or there's a sudden change in their feeding pattern, it's time to call the doctor.

Keep a close eye on fevers, persistent crying or irritability, especially if they're under a month old. Trust your instincts, and don't hesitate to call your baby's doctor for expert advice.

But, if things take a serious turn, like difficulty waking up, weakness, strange noises with each breath, or bluish lips, it's 911 time—no second thoughts.

On a less urgent note, any symptoms like coughing, diarrhea, vomiting, changes in feeding, excessive sweating during feeds, or unusual sleeping patterns warrant a call to the doctor. If you spot pink, orange, or peachy-colored urine or have any other concerns, touching base with the doctor within 24 hours is a good idea.

Now, take a deep breath. If your baby is feeding, moving, and sleeping like a champ, and there are no signs of illness, you're rocking this newborn journey!

7.2 COMMON BABY PHASES

You'll be amazed by the number of phases your baby will undergo in just 6 months.

Baby Acne

Baby acne is a common phase for many infants and occurs approximately 2-4 weeks from birth. It will look like small bumps commonly on the face or neck, like a rash. Thankfully, it's just a phase. And because it's hormonal and not linked to your diet or hygiene, and usually vanishes on its own. You can wash the area with warm water and a soft cloth or rub with breastmilk, but ideally, not much else. It should clear up within 2 weeks to 1 month.

Jaundice

Before leaving the hospital on day 4, my baby's skin took on a yellowish hue. Jaundice, they told me. The doctor reassured me that it's common in newborns, often due to their underdeveloped liver. After a bit of phototherapy, the jaundice gradually faded away.

Cradle Cap

Cradle Cap is another common baby phase your baby may experience in the first 2 months. A cradle cap causes crusty, flaky, or scaly patches on your baby's scalp or eyebrows. It's believed to be an overproduction of oil in the skin that interferes with the natural shedding of skin on your baby's scalp, causing a build-up of dead skin on the scalp. This is another condition that does not need treatment, can last a few weeks to months, and generally clears up on its own. Regardless, if you want to remove the crusty flakes, I was told you could massage olive oil into the scalp during bath time and rinse with a mild baby shampoo. You can brush the flakes with a soft bristle baby brush as they lift.

Eczema

Eczema also made an appearance in our journey, causing red, dry patches on my baby's sensitive skin. It most likely affected me more than him, but we learned that mild moisturizing and using products made for sensitive skin could alleviate the irritation. For stubborn areas that wouldn't go away, the pediatrician was able to prescribe stronger creams.

Fevers

And then there's the fever. Fever is the body's way of fighting infections and is very common in children as they get used to the outside world.

Babies can develop fevers for various reasons, but it's frightening, nonetheless. And while fevers in children are common, knowing when you're in the danger zone is helpful.

For newborns up to 3 months, any temperature above 100.4°F (38°C) is a red flag and should be taken to the pediatrician. Between 3 and 6 months, a temperature of 101°F (38.3°C) or higher could be considered a reason to see the doctor.

As your baby ages from 6 months to a year, you'll become more accustomed to the fever scares. However, a temperature surpassing 102°F (38.9°C) is worth paying attention to, and it's always best to check if you're worried.

Signs of a fever:

- Appearing unwell (irritable or crying)
- Hot to touch
- Shivering
- Vomiting
- Refusing to drink
- More sleepy than usual

There are many types of thermometers, so choose one that you're comfortable with and suitable for young babies.

There is no need to give your baby medicine for a fever unless they are in pain or discomfort. The key is to monitor them, keep them comfortable and hydrated.

Here are a few tips to help make them more comfortable:

- Keep them hydrated by offering extra formula or breast milk
- Baby pain reliever
- Cool, wet cloth on their forehead
- Monitor their clothing so they're not too hot or cold

Take your baby to the pediatrician if:

- Temperature is above 100.4°F (38°C)
- Vomiting or refusing to drink
- Seem sleepier than usual or are experiencing breathing problems
- Fever lasts more than 2 days
- Seem to be getting worse

Remember, these are just general guidelines. Trust your instincts! You know your child best. If in doubt, don't hesitate to contact your pediatrician. Fevers can be scary, but with a bit of knowledge and a dash of parental intuition, you'll navigate them like a pro.

Viruses

I felt so bad when my little one got his first cold. His little nose was blocked, and he would constantly wake himself at night as most babies are nose breathers. This clearly warranted a visit to the pediatrician. Thankfully, it was just a virus, and I followed the required steps by spraying his nose with nasal spray and draining it with a mucus sucker. Regardless, I needed that reassurance and found that with each visit, I gained more confidence in dealing with any issue and recognizing when it's genuinely worrisome.

To all you first-time moms out there, please remember this: these common baby phases might be unsettling, but they are part and parcel of the beautiful journey of motherhood. Have faith in your instincts, seek advice when necessary, and savor these fleeting moments because they pass by all too swiftly. You've got what it takes to navigate this path!

7.3 UMBILICAL CORD CARE

For most moms, the umbilical cord is cut and clamped after birth, leaving the umbilical stump, which is still attached to your baby. Within days, the umbilical stump will get darker, dry up, and eventually fall off. This can take 1-2 weeks; however, it's important to let the stump fall off independently. Do not try to pull it off, even if it looks ready.

Taking care of your baby's umbilical cord stump helps prevent infection. Use only water to keep it clean unless it is exposed to pee or poo, in which case a mild baby cleanser can be used.

Keep the stump dry and exposed to air as much as possible. Fold the top part of the diaper below the stump, as this will help with the healing process. Once the stump has fallen off, keep the area dry and clean until it has healed completely.

Some oozing around your baby's belly button is normal during the healing process, but if you notice any red areas, puss, or an unpleasant smell, this could be a sign of an infection, so it's best to check with your pediatrician.

7.4 DIAPERING ESSENTIALS

The world of diapering can feel overwhelming with its array of products but fear not; I'm here to help you navigate it. Let's break down what you truly need:

Diapers

Whether you go for cloth or disposable, these are essential. Be prepared for 10-12 diaper changes daily in the first month. That's around 300-370 diapers for the month. Also, be sure to choose the right size for your baby's age and weight.

Changing Table & Pad

Invest in a sturdy changing table at the right height to avoid straining your back. A soft changing pad is a must; don't forget a washable changing pad cover.

Diaper Caddy

Keep things organized with a caddy, storing diapers, wipes, rash cream, and a distraction toy.

Wipes

Go for soft, hypoallergenic wipes. A wipe warmer can add a touch of luxury to your baby.

Diaper Pail

This is your odor-fighting hero, designed to keep the nursery smelling fresh.

Hand Sanitizer

An essential for quick hand sanitizing during and between diaper changes.

Rash Cream

Even with the best care, diaper rash can happen, so keep a tube in your caddy and diaper bag.

Stocking Up

Expect to use 8-12 diapers daily for the first few months, which adds up to about 3,000 diapers in the first year.

Choosing the Perfect Diaper

Consider type, fit, absorbency, material, and cost when choosing between cloth and disposable diapers.

Diaper Bag Must-Haves

In your diaper bag, make sure to include diapers, wipes, extra baby clothes, hand sanitizer, a small bottle if bottle feeding, a changing pad, and a rash cream.

Wee & Poo is a Good Thing

As a new parent, you may wonder how often your newborn should have wet diapers. In those initial days, you can expect your baby to have approximately one wet diaper per day of life. However, as the first week progresses, you should see a shift to about six to eight wet diapers in 24 hours.

This increase in wet diapers indicates that your baby is getting the nourishment and hydration they need to thrive. As a new mom, I found comfort in this simple yet essential sign of my baby's well-being.

In the same capacity, you want to make sure your baby is pooping as well!

Monitoring Your Baby's Poo

Explore the fascinating realm of baby poop: a topic that might seem a bit peculiar to fixate on but trust me, it becomes a pretty big deal in parenting.

In those early days, your baby's poop will go through a series of changes. The first poop, meconium, is a sticky, tar-like substance that can catch you off guard. But don't worry; it transitions into a mustard-yellow shade soon enough.

For breastfed babies, the poop often resembles fancy mustard which is perfectly normal. When you switch to formula, the poop parade might slow down a bit. It tends to be a bit thicker and might even take on a different color. But, surprise, surprise! Shades of brown, yellow, and green are all fair game.

The frequency of poop in the early days can vary greatly. Believe it or not, when my son was about 3 months old, he didn't poop for over a week! Safe to say, I was concerned, but my pediatrician assured me that it was entirely normal, especially if it was not causing distress.

Solid foods make their entrance around 6 months, introducing a whole new level of excitement. Suddenly, you're analyzing textures and colors like a detective. Don't panic if you see undigested bits; it's just your baby's system adjusting.

Remember, every baby is different, and their poop will be too. If you notice anything genuinely concerning or your instincts kick in, call your pediatrician. But for the most part, embrace the weird and wonderful world of baby poop. It's a messy, smelly adventure, but it's all part of the parenting journey!

7.5 BATHING ESSENTIALS

When it comes to bathing your baby, it's crucial to remember that you should never leave your little one unattended. Drowning is the number one cause of death for children under the age of 4. Therefore, your supervision is of the utmost importance.

As a mom, I understand how challenging it can be to remember everything you need for bath time, especially when dealing with the infamous mom brain. So, for those of you who appreciate having a handy checklist for baby bath time, here it is, with all the essentials:

For a newborn's bath, you'll require:

Baby Bathtub or Bath Seat

Once your baby's umbilical cord falls off, you can give them their first bath in the sink or a bathtub. You can use a sink insert, a baby bathtub, or a bath seat that fits in your regular bathtub. Personally, we liked the baby bathtub because we could just place on the countertop and our son could float in the tub and relax.

Washcloth

Baby washcloths are smaller and thinner than regular ones.

Bath Thermometer

The ideal temperature for newborns is approx. 97 degrees Fahrenheit. It should feel comfortably warm but not hot.

Body Wash/Shampoo

For very young babies, plain water is sufficient, but as they grow, you'll want to use some baby body wash and shampoo.

Toothbrush/Baby Oil

If your baby has a cradle cap, you can gently brush their head with a soft toothbrush and add baby oil if needed.

Small Hand Towel

This is a favorite trick of mine. Cover your baby with a small hand towel in the tub to keep them warm and secure. You can gradually uncover parts of them as you wash them and then re-cover them with the warm, wet blanket.

Rinsing Cup

You can purchase an official rinsing cup or use an old cup, water bottle, or even your hands.

Bath Kneeler

This is a cushioned mat to kneel on and save your knees during bath time.

Towel

Baby towels are not only practical but also incredibly cute. Just make sure to put a diaper on your baby before you get carried away taking photos!

Lotion

If your baby has minor eczema, applying lotion right after bath time can be helpful.

Clean Diapers and Clothes

Be sure to have clean diapers and a fresh outfit ready to go.

Warm Blanket

After the bath, I like to wrap my baby in a cozy, fuzzy blanket to help them warm up while I cuddle or feed them.

For older babies, the bath time supply list remains similar but includes some extra items:

- Space Heater (if needed): If the room is a bit chilly, running a small space heater in the bathroom before starting the bath ensures your baby stays cozy and warm.
- Washcloth
- Spout and Drain Covers (optional): These covers prevent bumps and protect your baby during bath time.
- Bathmat: This mat goes at the bottom of the bathtub, making it less slippery. I consider it an essential addition.
- Bath Toys & Storage Caddy: These are not only fun but also practical. You can invest in a storage caddy as well.

So, whether you're bathing a newborn or an older baby, follow this checklist and enjoy these precious moments with your little one. Bath time is not just about keeping your baby clean; it's also an excellent opportunity to bond and make beautiful memories.

Bathing Position

The ideal bath temperature is about 97 degrees Fahrenheit (36 degrees Celsius). Place your baby into the bath. Your baby will be fully supported by either your left or right arm, leaving the other arm free to wash, play, rinse, or adjust the washcloth. Place your left arm under your baby's head and wrap your left hand around your baby's shoulder, creating a hold with your thumb and middle finger. Your baby's head will be supported by the underside of your forearm, keeping their head above water.

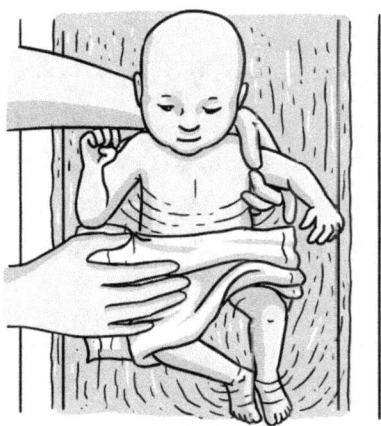

7.6 ROUTINE CHECK-UPS

Routine check-ups for your baby are a crucial part of their early life. I remember those first few visits to the pediatrician with my little one, feeling excitement and nervousness.

In the early days, you'll have those initial visits just after birth, which usually involve checking your baby's weight, height, head circumference, and general well-being. These appointments help ensure your baby is growing and developing as they should. You might also discuss feeding, sleep patterns, and any concerns you have as a new mom. I recall asking many questions during these visits, seeking reassurance and guidance.

As the months go by, you'll continue with regular check-ups. These visits serve as milestones for your baby's development. Don't be surprised if you document those early milestones in a baby journal or create a digital baby album. I did the same, capturing those precious moments like first steps and words. These memories will stay with you forever.

To help you do this, I created a FREE BABY MILESTONE TRACKER which can be downloaded at the front of this book. My gift to you as a THANK YOU for purchasing my book.

Your pediatrician can advise exactly when these regular check-ups are needed as it's usually based on their age or the vaccinations required. It will most likely be three days, two weeks, two months, four months, and six months. If you're worried about forgetting, book all appointments for the first six months ahead of time, and you're set!

The routine check-ups generally reassure your baby's development is 'on track.' But if you have any concerns or questions, also offer a chance to address them. It's time for open communication with your pediatrician, who can provide valuable insights and recommendations based on their expertise.

7.7 VACCINATIONS

Vaccinations are a personal choice for every first-time mom, and there is much to consider. Doing your own research combined with your baby's doctor will be your best guide. Numerous vaccinations are recommended from birth to 2 years, so it's worth deciding beforehand.

7.8 EMERGENCY SITUATIONS

If you see any of the following symptoms, call 911 immediately.

- Severe drowsiness or unresponsiveness
- Difficulty breathing or unusual breathing
- Cold hands or feet or pale, blotchy, or blue skin
- Seizures
- A rash that doesn't fade when you press your child's skin

These symptoms must not be taken lightly, so seek medical help immediately. Hopefully, you never have to, but it's helpful to know. A useful resource is the American Academy of Pediatrics (app.org).

Newborn health is a rollercoaster but also a journey of discovery. Every hiccup and giggle is a milestone. So, first-time moms, embrace the chaos, savor the snuggles, and know you're doing an amazing job in this newborn adventure.

The next chapter focuses on bonding with your baby. Of course, knowing how to care for your little one is crucial, but spending time and building a bond holds equal importance. So, let's learn more!

8

BONDING WITH YOUR BABY

"There are places in the heart you don't even know exist until you love a child."

— ANNE LAMOTT

Welcome to Chapter 8: an essential piece of your motherhood adventure. This chapter is all about the enchanting connection with your little one. Picture a symphony of baby giggles, warm snuggles, and a whole lot of bonding.

Let's start by exploring the significance of skin-to-skin contact. It's more than just a touch; it's a powerful language that is incredibly beneficial for you and your baby.

Onto babywearing— those carriers are more than just fashion statements; they're your secret weapon for multitasking while keeping your bundle of joy close. Imagine conquering grocery shopping with a sleeping baby strapped to you. It's a game-changer!

And then interactive playtime. From peek-a-boo to silly faces, prepare for a crash course in baby-approved entertainment that deepens your bond.

So, buckle up, new moms! Chapter 8 is your guide to transforming cuddles into unforgettable moments. Get ready to embark on this heart-warming journey of bonding with your little one in the first 6 months.

8.1 IMPORTANCE OF SKIN-TO-SKIN

Skin-to-skin contact is a beautiful way to connect with your newborn by placing them, perhaps just in a diaper and a cute beanie, directly on your bare chest. You can cover up with a cozy blanket, gown, or shirt for that extra warmth.

So, when can you start this snuggle fest? Moms, you can dive in right after delivery, whether it's a vaginal birth or a C-section. Your partner can dive right in as well, especially while you get some post-delivery TLC.

Have you heard of the golden hour? It's that magical first hour after birth when you and your baby are primed to form a chemical connection. Skin-to-skin contact during this time can do wonders for bonding and breastfeeding. But life happens, right? No stress if you can't do the skin-to-skin thing right after birth. There will be plenty of opportunities in the coming weeks and months.

Now, let's talk about benefits. Skin-to-skin isn't just a cozy cuddle; it's a power move. It regulates your baby's temperature, stabilizes their breathing and heartbeat, and promotes breastfeeding. And guess what? It's not just for moms. Dads, you're in on this bonding action too, and it can be done anytime from birth.

As for postpartum depression, studies suggest skin-to-skin might help keep it at bay. Again, dads don't think you're off the hook— your turn for some bonding and confidence boost. And if your baby is upset, skin-to-skin contact is a great way to calm them.

Safety first, though. If there are any medical hiccups, skin-to-skin might take a rain check. But there will be plenty of bonding time ahead for many months, and skin-to-skin is the superhero. Life might throw a curveball, but you've got this.

8.2 BABYWEARING

Have you ever noticed parents rocking various colorful baby carri-ers? Backpack-style or wraps, there's a whole world to explore. So, what's the scoop? Turns out, babywearing, as they call it, is a game-changer for both you and your baby. Fun fact: different cultures worldwide have been rocking baby-wearing for ages.

Back in '86, a study found that carried babies cried and fussed less, especially during the evening hours. There are health benefits to this. Skin-to-skin contact is a hit in hospitals, especially for premature babies. Babywearing, with the right carrier, can regu-late heartbeat, temperature, and breathing patterns.

Breastfeeding parents, take note. While research on the link between baby-wearing and breastfeeding is still in the works, you can feed on the go if you're into that.

Connection time! Baby-wearing undoubtedly promotes bonding with your baby. And the bonus? It's hands-free! Daily tasks become a breeze: fold laundry, read to an older sibling, or take a stroll downtown. Just skip the deep frying or skateboarding; that's a bit much.

Now, safety first. There's a right way to do babywearing, and it involves remembering this: Keep the baby tight, in view, close enough to kiss, chin off chest, and with a supported back. Comfort for you matters, too.

So, what's your carrier of choice? From soft wraps to structured carriers, it depends on your baby's age, body type, and personal preferences. As I mentioned earlier, it's a good idea to have a breathable wrap when babywearing indoors and a more structured carrier when outdoors.

Follow the manufacturer's directions for the correct positions based on your baby's weight. Typically, babies start facing you, then eventually face out, and as they grow, back-carrying becomes an option.

Oh, and twins? Yep, you can wear them too! Two carriers or a woven wrap are options. In a nutshell, baby-wearing isn't just a trend; it's a lifestyle. It keeps your baby close while allowing you to tackle your to-do list. So, grab that carrier and get ready for a hands-free adventure.

8.3 INTERACTIVE PLAYTIME

You, my friend, are not just a mom but also the go-to playmate and the very first teacher for your little one.

In the beginning, playtime is somewhat limited. Newborns have a knack for sleeping, and when they're awake, you're deep in the feeding and caring routine. As your baby's awake windows start to increase, as set out in Chapter 4, and the feeding time decreases, you'll have more playtime with each other.

Regardless, babies are born ready to communicate with you, and regular play with your newborn helps their brain develop. Interactive playtime not only promotes physical activity but also supports cognitive development, social skills, and emotional well-being. I'll go into more detail in Chapter 10 when discussing your baby's first milestones.

There are great brands such as Lovevery that create Play Kits designed specifically for babies at a certain age. They work with child development experts to give you an array of toys to help facilitate their brain development, along with additional DIY toys you can create at home.

Now, interaction levels vary for every baby. Some chill, gazing at their toes, while others crave more action. Babies drop hints through sounds, expressions, and movements. Diaper changes? Yep, they count as quality time. Give your baby lots of smiles and songs while they're on the change table.

Spot moments to place them on a safe play mat with toys. Do your thing nearby and let them explore. Gradually extend their me time over weeks, staying close and picking them up before the fussing kicks in.

Here are a few ideas to engage with your baby to promote healthy childhood development:

Birth to 3 months:

- *Imitation:* Imitate your baby's coos, sounds, and expressions. It lets them know you're paying attention, and it makes them feel important.
- *Cycling:* Lay your baby on their back and move their legs in a cycling motion. This helps strengthen your baby's abdominal muscles but also the alternating motion that

will be valuable when it comes time to crawl and walk. It also relieves gas as a bonus!

- *Eye-Catching Mobiles* – Babies can't see very far at this age, so mesmerizing mobiles are great to spark their curiosity. Consider playmats with an arching mobile in which you can swap different toys every few weeks to keep your baby engaged.
- *Balance* – Hold your baby securely on top of a beach ball or yoga ball and gently roll them back and forth while describing what you're doing.
- *Black & White Images* – A newborn's vision isn't fully developed, making high-contrast images in black and white the best form of imagery in the first few months. There are plenty of soft baby books with this design in mind, or print off several simple, black and white images and place them around your house.
- *Mirror Play* – Mirrors are extremely engaging for babies. Most baby toys have a mirror installed, which is great as a visual during tummy time, or feel free to hold your baby up in front of a mirror.
- *Sensory Play* – Exploring various textures is always fun for babies. Look around the room to find a few baby-safe objects that you can run your baby's hand over.
- *Reading Together* – There's nothing more precious than holding your baby and reading to them. They will love your cuddles but also hear your voice, so be sure to make this a ritual during each playtime.
- *Swing Together* – If you're passing by a swing set, feel free to jump on a swing together! Popping them in a baby carrier is the best way to enjoy swinging together.

- *Airplane* – Hold your baby face down under your arm, giving them a new perspective and relieving some gas (if needed). Gently sway side to side and make airplane noises.
- *Massage* – Massage is a brilliant way to support your baby's circulatory and digestive systems. Use gentle pressure and apply edible oils such as grapeseed, almond, or olive oil.
- *Conversation Time* – Support your baby's language development by talking to them constantly. The easiest way to do this is to describe everything you're doing.
- *Dance Together* – Another activity that might be easier with an indoor baby carrier. Pop on some tunes, maybe choose a different theme each day and dance around the room together.
- *Stimulated Play* – Knowing babies enjoy high contrast and moving objects, play with a flashlight in a darkened room.
- *Introduce Smell* – While your baby cannot voluntarily smell yet, feel free to pass pleasant scents such as vanilla, citrus fruits, or flowers under their nose.
- *Eye Contact* – Take a few minutes to make meaningful eye contact with your baby to foster attachment and introduce nonverbal communication.
- *Stretch* – Time to break free from the fetal position! Try gently stretching your baby's arms and legs, one at a time.
- *Baby Sit-ups* - Lay your baby on a blanket, grasp the top corners of the blanket near their head, and bring your baby towards you. Slowly lay them back down and repeat a few times. This is designed to help strengthen your baby's neck muscles.

After 3 months, your baby officially passed the fourth trimester, is less sleepy, and, consequently, more engaged! Here are some activities for the next 3 months!

3 to 6 months:

- *Bubbles* – Bubbles will be a great activity for years to come, but at this age, it will help your baby practice reaching, hand-eye coordination, and eye tracking when following the bubble in various directions.
- *Loud and Soft Sounds* – Now is a good time to introduce loud and soft sounds. The best way is to sing to your baby at various volumes. Maybe sing the chorus loudly and the verse softly.
- *Baby and Me classes* – Your baby will continue to develop their neck and core strength, so this is a great time to do some Baby and Me classes. See if your local gyms offer this or try some classes on YouTube so you can get your workout on!
- *Big Kid Play* – Take your baby to the park so they can watch what the big kids are doing!
- *Ice Texture Play* – Set up a baking tray of ice cubes and let your baby feel the ice and move it around the tray as it melts. This is perfect for tummy time; just prop them up on a pillow so they can move their hands more freely.
- *Water Play* – Similar to the ice cube, try to prop your baby up with a pillow for tummy time and place water in a tray with several different objects they can play with.
- *Footsies* – While your baby is on their back, hold objects up to their feet and encourage them to kick the objects. This works well with activity play mats.
- *Talking time* – As always, continue to talk, talk, talk. Keep exposing your baby to as much language as possible. This activity never goes out of style!
- *Tummy Time in the Air* – A great twist on tummy time is to lay on your back with your knees to your chest. Place your baby on your shins, hold their hands, and have them fly in

the air on your legs. This will give your baby much more
to look at and tick the daily tummy time box.

These are just a few suggestions to help promote their development and strengthen your bonding time. And remember, babies
have a short attention span. Signs of stimulation overload include
eye-rubbing, looking away, or some good old fussing.

Thankfully, babies need their solo time to slowly figure out their
independence, so you don't need to watch them like a hawk during
every playtime. Regardless, it's a beautiful sight to watch them
grow and develop new skills every day.

So, dive into the wonderful world of baby play. It's a mix of fun,
bonding, and letting your little explorer spread their wings. All in
a day's work!

8.4 TUMMY TIME

Looking back, I didn't realize how important tummy time was.
Turns out, it's extremely important and should be a daily ritual,
even if it's just a few minutes.

Tummy time helps your baby develop their neck, shoulder, and
arm muscles, which are needed to help them sit up, crawl, and
eventually walk. Simply put, everything becomes a bit easier when
they can support their own neck. They feel less fragile and are on
their way to developing those key muscles needed for the next big
milestones.

Not all babies enjoy tummy time. They will express frustration, a
bit of wiggling, and maybe a tiny protest. But here's the secret:
make it fun! I used to get down on the floor with my baby, creating
a tummy time zone with colorful toys, soft blankets, and a whole
lot of encouragement. We did the tummy time gig on the bed, the

living room floor, anywhere with a comfy surface. It became our little bonding ritual.

And you know what the experts say about tummy time helping prevent the flat head situation? Well, it worked like a charm for us. My little explorer was building strength, developing motor skills, and getting a front-row seat to the wonders around them all while on their tummy.

So, dear first-time moms, don't stress about the clock ticking during tummy time. Make it a joyous routine, and before you know it, your baby will be acing tummy time like a pro, turning those mini push-ups into a celebration of milestones. Cheers to the tummy time journey!

And another one bites the dust! This chapter covered all the various aspects of baby bonding. From the importance of skin-to-skin contact to interactive playtime, I shared my experiences and tips to help you navigate these joyful moments with your little one!

So, now that you know how to spend time with your baby, how about we skip to taking care of ourselves? After all, the real journey begins postpartum!

POSTPARTUM CARE FOR MOMS

"A mother is always the beginning. She is how things begin."

— *AMY TAN*

T his chapter is meant to guide you through the special difficulties and rewards of being a new mother. We'll examine the physical healing process, traversing what frequently seems unfamiliar ground while revealing how to manage your emotional well-being.

9.1 PHYSICAL RECOVERY

It can be easy to give your kid your whole attention now that you're at home with them, but it's important to remember that your body also needs care after such a big event.

Your body has experienced a transformation, regardless of how smooth or erratic your delivery was. Postpartum healing is a lengthy process that takes several months to complete. Although many women report feeling better after 6 to 8 weeks, don't give up if it takes longer for you. The best course of action is to give your body the rest, nourishment, and care it deserves because it has its own schedule.

Those first several weeks, I recall feeling like my body was operating on a strange frequency. My hormones were in full swing, causing me to feel emotional and a little disoriented. Just remember that it's a necessary step in the process if you find yourself in a similar circumstance. Remember to be kind to yourself; these emotions will pass.

During this postpartum period, being mindful of your body's cues is important. While it's second nature to become engrossed in your baby's delight, paying attention to changes in your body to ensure a speedy recovery is essential.

Throughout these first several weeks, rest is your best friend. It will be more than sufficient if all you can do is take care of your child, eat, and sleep. And resist the urge to believe anything less.

Your doctor will advise you on what activities to avoid if you have a C-section. Certain things should be avoided, such as driving and lifting anything larger than your child for a while.

Postpartum recovery includes everything from constipation to hormonal changes, soreness in unexpected locations, and abdominal problems. Postpartum recovery is different for everyone, so while some discomfort is common, you should constantly be on the lookout for any strange or intensifying symptoms.

The baby blues, which affect between 70 and 80 percent of new mothers, may appear. Though it's quite an emotional rollercoaster, don't be afraid to get help if these feelings last or get intense. In this, you're not alone, and asking for assistance shows strength rather than weakness.

Oh, the delights of postpartum: perineum discomfort, hemorrhoids, hormonal changes, and swollen nipples. Recall that these are just transient conflicts and self-care is the best thing you can give yourself.

Sore breasts and nipples may be a common early experience for nursing moms. If necessary, get advice from lactation specialists and keep in mind that there is no one-size-fits-all nursing method.

Are you experiencing stitches or staples left over following C-sections or episiotomies? Take it easy and follow the advice of your physician. Cleaning the area is essential, and healing time frames vary.

Your body is trying to reset, so expect vaginal bleeding and discharge for a bit. Although a certain amount of water retention is typical, excessive edema must be watched. Because of all your body has been through, have patience and concentrate on caring for yourself while you nurse.

For those of you who had a C-section, keep in mind that your recuperation will be different in several ways. It's important to adhere to the instructions provided by your doctor. Watch the area around your incision and contact your doctor immediately if you see any redness, swelling, or seeping pus. The underlying stitches could take up to 12 weeks to heal, while the visible ones should take 5–10 days.

Finally, and possibly above all, pay attention to your body. Don't ignore feelings that seem strange. Speak with your doctor if you're experiencing any worrying symptoms, such as excessive bleeding, ongoing headaches, or any other symptoms. Your well-being is important for the sake of you and your baby.

Remind yourself that you are a superhero deserving of all the love and care in the world, not just a mom. You can do this!

9.2 EMOTIONAL WELL-BEING

Let's talk about the emotional tornado you may be going through. You might have experienced an intense mixture of relief, wonder, and delight immediately following your child's birth. When you go home, the emotions could change to overload, uncertainty, frustration, or anxiety.

Taking care of a newborn is a challenging task. It might be difficult to get used to the pandemonium they bring, and taking care of their demands all the time can be extremely draining. No matter how well-prepared you believe yourself to be, there will be highs and lows over the first few weeks and months.

Overnight, your days (and nights) have changed drastically. You used to be able to sleep when you wanted, go for a walk when you wanted, essentially, do anything you wanted, anytime. Now, that's not the case. You're on a looping schedule of sleeping, feeding, changing diapers, and entertaining your bundle. Safe to say, this schedule may be a shock to your system and your mental health. And that's completely understandable.

Please know that most women feel this, too. We experience this drastic change in our schedule, and while we wouldn't change it for the world, we can't ignore the need to adjust.

My suggestion would be to avoid making any big decisions right now. This means focusing on you and the baby. Let your partner look after you and hopefully handle most of the housework.

Focus on yourself and your baby. You've just taken on a huge responsibility; you're most likely sleep-deprived, and your day-to-day ritual has changed overnight. Everything else can wait. You've earned this time with your baby.

Onto the baby blues! Eight out of ten new mothers report feeling emotional, impatient, or tired after giving birth; these sentiments often peak three or four days later. Positive news? Usually, they disappear within two weeks.

Let's talk about postpartum depression, which affects around 1 in 5 new mothers. It can appear any time within the first year after birth and usually does so during the fourth week. Postpartum depression can be exacerbated by fatigue, overwhelm, and a loss of identity during the healing process.

You may experience symptoms such as anxiety, weariness, depression, or even dread of hurting your child or yourself. These emotions don't go away independently, so getting support and assistance is essential. Medication, talk therapy, or a combination of the two are available as forms of treatment. Never be afraid to discuss your struggles with your healthcare professional.

Meanwhile, take care of yourself, don't put too much pressure on yourself, seek assistance, talk to friends and family, get outside, spend time with your spouse, join a support group, and avoid making significant life changes at this delicate period.

9.3 GETTING BACK INTO SHAPE

Becoming the best mother, you can be is a never-ending roller coaster that includes sleepless nights, emotional highs and lows, and constant juggling. Oh, and don't forget about how your physique has changed; quite the contrast from nine months ago.

Here's the lowdown before you go into panic mode: it is totally possible to get back into shape after having a baby, but you shouldn't rush the process. Hear it from someone who has experienced it. These six suggestions will help you return to your pre-pregnancy figure or perhaps even surpass it!

Give Your Body Time

Being a new mum is an amazing job. You shouldn't get right into a strict diet or exercise regimen because your body recently went through a lot. Your greatest allies will be self-love, good habits, and patience.

Move Gradually

After your physician gives the all-clear, begin with quick strolls. Workouts that are intense can wait at least six weeks following childbirth. Increase the frequency of your 20–30-minute walks after your 6-week check-up.

Breastfeed

Not only is breastfeeding excellent for your infant, but it also burns an additional 800 calories every day. Not to mention that you require an additional 500 calories for yourself. Select nutrient-dense meals instead of empty-calorie snacks.

Accept Sleep

For new mothers, sleep deprivation is their worst enemy. It disrupts your metabolism, raises cravings, and lowers energy levels. When your infant sleeps, sneak in a nap; your body will thank you.

Eat Wisely

Now that the pregnancy has ended, it's time to set new dietary guidelines. Make breakfast your top priority, eat smaller, more balanced meals throughout the day, including fiber and protein, add healthy fats, and consume abundant fresh fruits and vegetables.

Resuming Exercise Gradually

Congratulations if you continued working out during your pregnancy! If not, no big deal; get started as soon as you feel ready, but take it steady. Use bridge and plank exercises to strengthen your core, incorporate yoga for flexibility, progressively resume cardio, and remember to use weights for general strength.

Here's something I did: I tried a postpartum Pilates class where I could bring my child. They were just lounging on the mat next to me. Seek something comparable nearby or enroll in an online course from home.

Don't forget about pelvic floor exercises. Since these muscles are under a lot of strain during pregnancy and childbirth, it's important to strengthen them to prevent any bladder or bowel problems.

Recall that it is a journey rather than a race. Although the weight may not go away immediately, if you follow these suggestions and have patience, success will come!

Now that we have tackled all that there is to postpartum recovery, it is time to move on to tracking your baby's milestones!

10

BABY'S FIRST MILESTONES

"A mother always has to think twice, Once for herself, and once for her child."

— SOPHIA LOREN

Being a parent is a unique experience, and getting to know your child is both a requirement and an adventure. The nuances of your baby's world are examined in this chapter, giving you an in-depth feel of what they are experiencing, what they need, and what to look for during their development.

I wanted to feel like I was doing everything possible to encourage my baby in all areas of development. Together, we'll examine your child's development month by month and offer advice on the finest toys and activities for their growth and enjoyment while fostering their individuality!

Understand Your Baby

Your baby is born ready to communicate, expressing their needs and preferences primarily through crying and body language. As you observe, remember that it's a two-way learning process; your baby is keenly observing you, too.

Your baby's development also begins at birth. Providing love, cuddles, and responding to their needs from day one will help their brain grow and develop.

Milestones are considered a way of tracking your baby's development. They are typically grouped into categories such as large body movements, small body movements, vision, hearing, speech and language, and social behavior and understanding.

All babies develop at their own rate, but there are general guidelines to keep in mind to ensure your baby is on the right track. If you suspect a delay in development of any kind, consult your pediatrician immediately.

Here are some general guidelines you can expect in the first six months:

10.1 MONTH ONE MILESTONES

As mentioned earlier, babies will lose weight right after birth, but typically gain this back within the first 2 weeks. Try not to compare your baby's weight gain to other babies, just make sure they are gaining weigh consistently.

Physical Development

Month one is centered around feeding, sleeping and skin-to-skin contact. Their behavior is caused by reflexes with a focus on sucking, swallowing, and searching for milk. They will also grasp objects or fingers that are placed in their hands but don't be surprised if their hands are clenched into a tight fist most of the time.

They can even start to put one foot in front of the other if placed on a flat surface. Their neck muscles will get stronger by the end of month one allowing them to lift their head during tummy time and even to one side.

Cognitive Development

Your baby will begin to focus and will be able to follow a moving object.

Social Development

Your face and voice will be the best toy for them at this age, and they will begin to recognize you.

Emotional Development

Your baby will use their crying voice to indicate their needs, whether hungry or uncomfortable. Imitate your baby's sounds back to them. Some babies will learn to soothe themselves by sucking a pacifier or their fingers. Sucking is a natural way for your baby to calm themselves.

What You Can Do

This is the time to connect with your baby. Looking deep into their eyes and smile to help form this beautiful bond of safety and security.

Read, sing, and play with your baby. They won't be able to fully understand but it's all part of the bonding process and stimulates their senses.

Tummy time when they are awake is pivotal. Aim for one to five minutes and do not leave them unattended.

Signs of Delayed Development

- Your baby isn't feeding well
- They are sleeping more than 16 hours a day
- They are not actively moving both arms and legs
- They are not responding to moving objects, such as your face
- You sense their hearing is off, such as not startled to loud noises
- Your suspect an issue with their crying or sleeping

10.2 MONTH TWO MILESTONES

Your baby is starting to grow quickly, and they may be putting on a lot of weight looking round and chubby. As their muscles develop, they will start to stretch their arms and legs. You can expect a growth spurt at about 6 weeks which will naturally result in fussiness and increased hunger. Respond to their cues and always feed them if they indicate hunger.

Physical Development

Your baby is now discovering their fingers and hands, allowing them to grasp an object, even if they don't let go. Your baby will also begin to coordinate their movements, shifting from jerky movements to smoother ones.

They'll begin to kick their legs and possibly even roll over. Therefore, never leave your baby unattended on a change table.

Tummy time will get more and more productive. You may see your baby move their head from side to side and even lift their chest off the ground.

Cognitive Development

Your baby will start to follow you with their eyes and enjoy looking at more complex patterns and colors. They may get bored with the same activity.

Social Development

Your baby may start to sleep longer stretches at a time and be more alert during the day. They will love looking at your face, locking eyes, and you may start to see some smiles.

Language Development

Your baby will start making more sounds, seeming to listen and talk back to you. They will also turn towards sounds they hear.

What You Can Do

As your baby's awake time increases, interactive playtime will become more available to help them develop.

Continue to read, sing, and talk to your baby as often as possible. This will help develop their language and communication skills.

And be sure to keep up the smiling and tummy time! One to five minutes is still a good goal!

Signs of Delayed Development

- Your baby isn't smiling by 8 weeks
- They won't calm down, even if you try to comfort them
- Their fists are still clenched or floppy
- They aren't feeding properly
- They aren't startled by loud noises
- They don't watch things as they move
- They don't bring their hands to their mouth

10.3 MONTH THREE MILESTONES

Good news! The worst of the crying should be over, and your baby will have formed a strong attachment to you. Your baby may start sleeping 5 to 6 hours at night, but all babies are different.

Physical Development

Your baby will start to reach for things and try to put things in their mouth. Your baby will start to hold their head up while sitting and tummy time could result in a roll from front to back. They'll wave their arms and kick their legs more strongly. In the right position, they may start to push down on their legs as if to stand.

Cognitive Development

As their sense of touch develops, objects will become more interesting as they take a long look and start to rattle them.

Social Development

Their brain is growing fast, and they will begin to smile at strangers. But don't worry, they know who mom and dad are by sight and smell.

Emotional Development

Your baby will start to explore the world around them, especially their own fingers and toes. They will recognize your voice, respond to different expressions, and begin to laugh out loud.

What You Can Do

Reading, singing, and talking will be a constant as the foundations of language are built. Choose books with large, bright pictures that you can point to and talk about.

Upgrade tummy time by dangling a toy in front of them to further develop their neck and back muscles. Continue sensory play by giving your baby different textures to feel.

Signs of Delayed Development

- They won't calm down, even if you try to comfort them
- Their fists are still clenched or floppy
- They aren't feeding properly
- They aren't startled by loud noises
- They don't watch things as they move
- They don't bring their hands to their mouth
- They can't hold their head up during tummy time when pushing up

10.4 MONTH FOUR MILESTONES

By month four, your baby will be learning to coordinate their body, gaining more control with their vision, touch, and physical movement. Most of the crying will have subsided with more communication to replace it.

Most babies will have doubled their weight by now and are starting to take an interest in the world, possibly showing an interest in food.

Physical Development

Your baby will start to pick up objects and continue to put just about everything in their mouth. They are getting ready for solid food but always monitor what they put in their mouth to avoid the risk of choking.

Their physical skills are developing with rolling over and sitting up not far off.

Cognitive Development

Your baby will start to link what they see to what they hear, taste, and smell.

Social Development

The interaction should be super fun now with the smiles, laughs, talking, and eye contact.

Emotional Development

Emotions like anger and frustration will start to develop. They will also start to enjoy looking at their reflection in the mirror.

What You Can Do

You and your baby may start to benefit from a routine, doing things in a similar pattern each day. It helps them feel safe and secure.

Continuing to talk and read to your baby will help them learn about language and communication. Mix up the interaction with different tones and facial expressions. Just have fun with songs, books, and toys, and be as animated as you'd like!

Signs of Delayed Development

- They don't recognize you
- Not making any voice sounds
- Are not interested in things around them
- They do not open their fingers
- Bent legs or not kicking their legs
- Not responding to your voice

- Appear to be unhappy or unsettled
- Your baby can't hold their head up

10.5 MONTH FIVE MILESTONES

By month five, your baby is learning more about the world and their place within it. Starting solids is just around the corner, as it's recommended to begin at 6 months.

At this stage, they are developing rapidly now. The good news is that you have nothing to worry about as long as they grow and gain weight as expected.

Physical Development

Your baby might be very close to sitting up on their own. Even if they can sit unsupported for a moment, stay close and place cushions around them in case they fall.

Tummy time will include more arms and leg stretches, perhaps some rolls both ways. And while on their back, they may lift their head and shoulders, further showing how their strength is developing. Feel free to have some fun and bounce them up and down on your lap.

Cognitive Development

Activity mats will be fun at this age as they start to swipe objects with their hands. They will also shake objects in their hands and look at them with curiosity.

Social Development

Your baby may start to get good at expressing their needs, such as lifting their arms to be picked up or crying if you leave.

Emotional Development

Your baby is learning about cause and effect, so get ready for the repeat game! If they drop something and see you pick it up, they will want to do it again and again. You may also experience laughs, giggles, cuddles, and kisses from your baby, so enjoy it!

Language Development

Language skills are really starting to take shape now. Your baby may repeat a sound over and over, such as sticking their tongue out and blowing bubbles. They may recognize toys that make sounds, so distraction gets a bit easier.

What You Can Do

Engage in a conversation with your baby by responding to their sounds with different tones and facial expressions. Tell them what you're going to do, such as, "I'm going to change your diaper, or "We're going to have ten minutes of tummy time." This gives them comfort about what is happening.

Let your baby copy you, whether it be a facial expression such as sticking out your tongue or pushing a button on a toy. This helps them build confidence in what they can do on their own.

Floor time is excellent for helping them develop their strength. Place them in different positions on the floor so they can move and explore toys differently. Continue to vary their toys with different textures, but know they might go in their mouth, so be vigilant.

Signs of Delayed Development

- They aren't interested in you or things around them
- Isn't learning to make sounds
- Limited movement with their fingers or legs
- They don't follow an object with their eyes
- They don't respond to your voice
- Appear to be unhappy or unsettled

10.6 MONTH SIX MILESTONES

You made it to six months! It's an exciting time because your baby's left side of the brain has started to communicate with the right side of the brain, giving better full-body coordination.

You and your baby will have a good understanding of each other and your ability to respond to their cues. They'll also be able to distinguish familiar faces from strangers. They'll even react to their own name.

Introducing solids at 6 months is recommended as it gives them the additional nutrients they need but also builds jaw strength to help them chew food and talk. Solids can be introduced as pureed, mashed, or intact via baby-led weaning. I'll discuss this more in Chapter 12.

Physical Development

Your baby's hand control will have developed enough to allow them to grab and move an object towards them. You may see them pass an object from one hand to the other and drop something with the understanding that it fell.

Most babies can roll both ways by now, so always keep a close eye on them while on the changing table. This means that they will start to push themselves up to a crawling position and perhaps begin to rock back and forth. Your baby will start to sit without support.

While standing with support, they may be able to push up and down with their legs and begin to turn in the direction they want to go.

Cognitive Development

Believe it or not, your baby may get bored if left alone for too long. Peek-a-boo is a great game at this age!

Social Development

Babies at this age love interaction and will learn to attract your attention in other ways than crying. They can most likely understand a few words often, such as 'bath,' so continue to give them the play-by-play about what's happening.

Emotional Development

Your baby is learning to understand emotions by the tone of your voice, such as a harsh or soft tone.

Language Development

You'll hear several sounds by this age, including babbling, singing, and bubble-blowing. Feel free to mimic these sounds to your baby in a conversational way to help them learn to talk.

What You Can Do

Babies this age want to explore everything around them, so set a safe play area with soft balls, teething rings, or noise makers.

Continue to talk and listen to your baby with good eye contact so they know you are present. Read to your baby combined with good cuddles. Reassure them when they're with anyone else, so they feel safe and secure.

It's a good idea to baby-proof your house as they could be on the move by now!

Signs of Delayed Development

- They don't recognize you
- Aren't making eye contact
- Aren't babbling or making sounds
- Not interested in toys or what's around them
- Not comforted by their primary caregiver
- Their body seems very stiff or floppy
- Do not respond to sounds around them
- Are not rolling in either direction
- Doesn't laugh or make squealing sounds
- Has difficulty getting things to their mouth

The early months are a time of discovery. As you can see, your face and voice become the best toys, and your interactions help your baby learn and communicate.

I also enjoyed the 'Baby Sparks' app which can be found on the Apple Store or Google Play Store. It offers daily play activities designed to support your baby's brain development, specifically from 0-3 years old. The videos demonstrate the activity and are said to benefit your baby if one for even a few minutes a day.

As you navigate this path, you'll find that your baby has unique preferences, and your responsiveness will build a strong parent-child connection. So, embrace the journey, trust your instincts, and enjoy this front-row seat in your baby's development!

10.7 BEST BABYTOYS FOR DEVELOPMENT

The journey of baby development is quite an adventure, and guess what? Toys play a crucial role! They aren't just playthings; they're the secret to your baby's sensory, motor, cognitive, and social-emotional growth.

Imagine this: toys with different textures, shapes, and colors working their magic, promoting brain development, and intro-ducing your baby to their world. Those cute little hands reaching, grasping, and manipulating toys. It's a workout for fine and gross motor skills, hand-eye coordination, and depth perception. And let's not forget the problem-solving skills – shape sorters and stacking toys are like little geniuses in disguise.

But there's more! Toys are the partners in crime for social-emotional development. Baby dolls and toy animals become mentors for empathy and social skills. Watch as your baby imitates adults, dives into pretend play, and becomes a creativity powerhouse.

Now, here's the fun part— some fantastic toys to light up your baby's development journey:

Baby Sensory and Fidget Toy

Made of food-grade silicone, this multitasking wonder is perfect for teething and exploration. Toggles, sounds, and vibrations; it's a sensory delight.

Interactive Book Toy

Turn pages, select activities; it is a smart toy for your little bookworm.

Interactive Puppy Toy

A battery-operated furball teaching words, body parts, counting, and the alphabet. Talk about a paw-some teacher!

Montessori Tissue Box

Endless fun pulling things out, a tissue box that keeps on giving.

Escape Crawling Crab

A fun companion for crawling adventures, eye-tracking, hand-eye coordination, and reaching milestones.

Wrist and Foot Rattles

Move and groove with these rattles! Perfect for motor development.

Baby Musical Instrument Set

A mini-Mozart in the making, which is great for motor and brain development. A collection of tambourines, rattles, maracas, xylophones, wrist bells, and clappers.

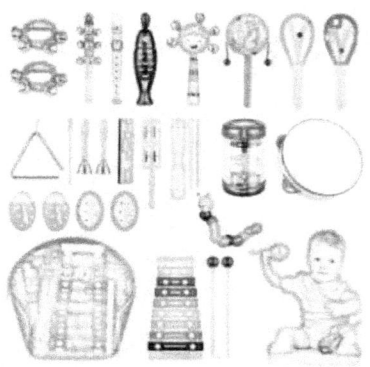

Piggy Bank Counting Toy

Teaching counting, playing songs, and introducing colors: a piggy bank with endless surprises.

Black and White Stimulating Mobile

Stimulating the brain with a strong contrast! A mobile that's easy on baby eyes. This can easily be swapped out for an activity mat.

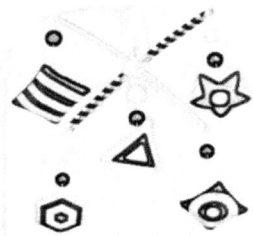

Tummy Time Floor Mirror

With tummy time being so important in the first few months, why not give them a mirror and toy they can engage with?

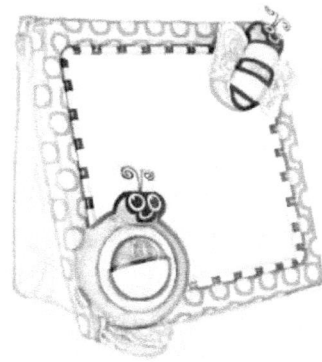

And there you have it! These toys are more than just play; they're steppingstones in your baby's incredible journey. Get ready for giggles, exploration, and a whole lot of developmental milestones!

10.8 MILESTONES TO LOOK FORWARD TO FROM NOW TO WALKING

Your baby will get better at what they're already doing, such as sitting without support. They will pick and throw small objects. They will begin to feed themselves with a spoon or grasp a cup to drink.

Typically, babies start walking between 10 and 18 months. Before this, there's the adorable crawling phase (around 7 to 12 months) and the "I'm standing up" show (usually between 9 and 12 months).

People say that it becomes more challenging once your baby starts walking, but I found it to be quite the opposite. They step into a new world, and they really start to explore on their own. Witnessing my little one take those initial unsteady steps was truly enchanting. I can imagine you eagerly awaiting that remarkable milestone, too!

Each stage of crawling, standing, and cruising are steppingstones to building muscle strength and refining skills like balance and coordination, all the essentials for the walking (and eventually, running) adventure!

Once those first steps occur, the journey doesn't halt. Babies experiment with standing, sitting, walking, and squatting, a workout routine that strengthens muscles and hones balance. They'll keep practicing, walking in different directions, on various surfaces, and sometimes even while carrying their favorite toys.

Now, how can you be the ultimate support system? Here are some ways!

- *Play Together:* Your presence is their safety net. Playing together builds confidence.
- *Encourage Independence:* Let them explore! It is a muscle-building and posture-perfecting adventure.
- *Distance Challenges:* Start with a short distance, then up the challenge by increasing the distance while monitoring them closely.
- *Obstacle Course Fun:* Soft cushions and foam shapes create a mini adventure park for those tiny feet.
- *Safe Home:* Clear the way! A safe environment ensures an accident-free exploration.

Trust me, those first steps are worth the wait. Enjoy the journey! It's a dance of milestones and memories!

And that was it for this chapter! The one thing that still mesmerizes me about babies is how fast they grow. Even though the process is fast, every milestone is fascinating and special.

Whether you're a working mom or a stay-at-home one, juggling everyday life as you embrace motherhood is nothing short of a challenge! Which is why the next chapter is about YOU!

BALANCING WORK, LIFE, AND MOTHERHOOD

"You're always going to wonder if you're doing things wrong, But that's what it means to be a mom, to care so much about someone else that you just want to be as perfect as possible."

— *NAYA RIVERA*

Becoming a mother is a life-changing decision. Previously, women had to choose between being a mother or having a career. Nowadays, women are fortunate enough to have both if they choose to. Whether you're a stay-at-home mom or a working mom, both have pros and cons. How will you feel going back to work? Can you find time for yourself?

Throughout this chapter, we'll delve into how to adjust to this new norm of motherhood, practical advice about returning to work with confidence, and strategies for maintaining your sanity amidst the chaos. But more than just surviving, it's about thriving in this new chapter of life!

11.1 ADJUSTING TO A NEW NORM

Adjusting to a new normal after welcoming a baby is a profound shift filled with joy and challenges. As a first-time mom, I vividly recall the transformative experience of finding my footing in this uncharted territory. The early days were a blend of sleepless nights and heart-melting moments, where each coo and tiny fingers grasping mine felt like a small miracle. Amidst the diaper changes and late-night feedings, a new routine emerged, and with it, a redefinition of what "normal" meant.

The spontaneity of pre-baby outings and uninterrupted sleep was replaced by a rhythm centered around the baby's needs. Initially overwhelming, this shift became an opportunity to discover a resilience I never knew existed. Adapting to an unpredictable schedule and functioning on limited rest became a badge of honor. Productivity took on a new definition, with small tasks becoming victories and time itself adopting a new dimension.

In navigating this new normal, finding joy in simple moments and embracing a slower pace became essential. Savoring quiet moments and recognizing the necessity of self-care reshaped my perspective on life. Challenges brought forth a support system: friends turned confidantes, family offering to help, and fellow moms sharing invaluable wisdom. These connections served as lifelines, a reminder that the journey into motherhood is not solitary.

Adapting wasn't without doubts and vulnerable moments. Questions about doing things right lingered, but with time, I learned to trust my instincts and appreciate the uniqueness of my parenting journey.

The new norm extended beyond adjusting to a baby's schedule; it was about embracing a profound transformation within myself. It involved learning that resilience and vulnerability could coexist, and that the messy, unpredictable moments held their own beauty.

To all first-time moms navigating this uncharted terrain, adjusting to the new norm is a journey of self-discovery. It's about finding strength in vulnerability, joy in simplicity, and building a support network that reminds you that you're not alone. Amid the unpredictable, you're crafting a story uniquely yours: a tale of love, growth, and the beautiful chaos that comes with being a mom.

11.2 GETTING OUT & ABOUT WITH CONFIDENCE

Stepping out with your baby can be a significant milestone, particularly for first-time moms. I still recall those initial days when the idea of leaving home with my little one sparked excitement and uncertainty. I didn't want him to get sick or cry profusely in front of others. However, through experience and a bit of trial and error, I discovered ways to make these outings more enjoyable and stress-free.

A light-hearted memory stands out. At approximately 3 months, I used to visit restaurants with my son when he was a baby. I'd strategically place my meal order while he was awake, and before the food arrived, I'd take him outside, rocking him to sleep. Juggling, holding him in one arm, and enjoying my dinner with the other, his short nap of about 45 minutes became the perfect window to relish a peaceful meal. It felt liberating to be out and about while still catering to his needs.

You'll quickly gain confidence in your ability to settle your child, no matter where you are. As long as they are near you, they will be happy. Take advantage of the stroller bassinet and baby carrier so both you and your baby can enjoy some fresh air.

Regarding travel, securing a baby bassinet on the plane can be a helpful tip. This thoughtful feature provides a comfortable space for your little one to rest during the journey, making the travel experience more manageable for both of you.

Another travel tip involves feeding your baby during take-off and descent. This simple act helps equalize the pressure in their ears, reducing discomfort during the flight. It's a small yet effective strategy to ensure a smoother experience for your baby.

Ultimately, gaining confidence in getting out with your baby is about discovering what works best for both of you. Whether it's creative dining strategies or travel hacks, the key is to embrace the adventure, learn from each experience, and relish the moments of joy that come with exploring the world with your little one.

11.3 RETURNING TO WORK

Returning to work after having a baby is like stepping into a new world filled with excitement and uncertainty. Likewise, returning to work doesn't diminish your role as a mom; it only adds another layer to your identity. Whether you're driven by career passion or financial necessity, the important thing is to trust your decision.

As first-time moms, we all struggle with the experience of leaving our little ones for the first time. Feeling a bit of guilt or separation anxiety is normal; these emotions are an integral part of the journey.

Here are a few tips to help navigate this challenging time:

Release the Working Mother's Guilt

Returning to work affects everyone differently. Letting go of guilt involves committing to self-compassion and understanding the reasons behind your choices. Remember that you are raising your child, and every choice you make is for them, whether you're physically present or not. Nowadays, women have the option to do both. Choose what makes you happy because your baby will be happy if you're happy.

Be Present Wherever You Are

It's important to feel like you're succeeding at work and motherhood. The way to do this is to be present when you're at work and be present when you're with your baby. Try not to let your personal life creep into work and vice versa. Otherwise, you won't be fully invested in either.

Find Good Childcare

Knowing that your baby is in good hands while you're at work is imperative. Finding someone you trust, whether a nanny, daycare program or assistance from family members, can help avoid additional mom guilt. Knowing your child is in a loving, caring, and supportive environment can provide priceless peace of mind.

Some daycares can have a waitlist of up to 1 year, so apply early if you need it.

Combine Calendars

The key to avoiding conflicts is to combine your work calendar and personal calendar. This way, you feel like you can achieve both, and one isn't being compromised by the other. Block off pumping time on your work calendar so meetings are not scheduled when you need to pump.

Connect with Other Moms

Working mothers might feel isolated due to societal expectations, but realizing they're not alone is crucial. Many women face similar challenges, regardless of marital status, work hours, or child age. So, joining parenting groups or workplace parenting support can provide a sense of community.

Engage in Honest Conversations with Your Boss

Although discussing your feelings with your boss might be challenging, it's often necessary. Communicate the difficulties of juggling work and newborn care. Suggest potential solutions or flexibility that can make the situation more manageable. Such as shifting hours to accommodate for daycare, or requesting a dedicated area to pump, or additional space in the fridge. An open dialogue benefits both parties.

Me-time Is Important

Ensure you eat well, spend quality time with your partner, indulge in leisure, and get sufficient sleep. These activities enhance productivity when you return to full-time work.

Celebrate Your Achievements

Motherhood is a fulfilling journey of balancing work and family responsibilities. Acknowledge your efforts and give yourself well-deserved recognition. Confidence in managing these dual roles deserves a pat on the back!

Returning to work after having a baby is a unique adventure: one that challenges and reshapes you. It's a process of rediscovery and growth, both personally and professionally. To all the first-time moms considering this journey, know that you have the strength to navigate through it.

Chapter 11 was all about discussing balance! Balancing is pretty much what motherhood is about; juggling life at home and work and getting out into the world after being cooped up in the new-mom life.

The last chapter will take us back to the baby! This time, we will jump to introducing foods to your little one.

A small confession: I've been one of those parents to have my baby taste a lemon and then proceed to record the most hilarious reaction! So much to look forward to. Keep reading!

INTRODUCING FOODS

"A mother's love endures through all."

— *WASHINGTON IRVING*

T he introduction of solid foods is a momentous occasion that is both exciting and unsettling. I'll share my own stories throughout this chapter in the hopes that they will speak to the feelings you're probably feeling.

We'll travel this path together, from that first spoonful to the messier times of baby-led weaning!

12.1 WHEN TO START SOLIDS

Healthcare professionals generally recommend waiting until your little one reaches around 6 months old before introducing solids; beginning before 4 months is advised against, just to ensure their system is ready. At the 6-month mark, babies usually need the additional nutrients found in solid foods, such as iron and zinc. It's also an ideal time to acquaint them with new tastes and textures.

While some babies might display signs of readiness before six months, like sitting up in a highchair, expressing interest in food, and not pushing food out of their mouths, it's essential to wait until they're at least 4 months old. If your baby is approximately double their birth weight, that's a good indicator, too.

12.2 ALLERGIES

Allergies need to be front of mind when starting solids. Ideally, introduce low-allergenic foods as your baby's first foods and gradually work with the more allergenic foods.

Once you have a handful of foods in the rotation that your baby doesn't have an issue with, gradually introduce one allergenic food at a time.

The top 9 allergenic foods are:

- *Chicken Eggs*
- *Peanuts*
- *Tree Nuts*
- *Sesame*
- *Fish*
- *Shellfish*
- *Soy*
- *Wheat*
- *Dairy/Cow's Milk*

It's recommended to offer your baby allergenic food in the morning as this gives you the most awake time to see if there is a reaction.

Remember to monitor for potential allergies one food at a time, with a few days in between.

Signs of an Allergic Reaction

The most common symptoms of a food allergy are:

- *Swelling of the lips, face, tongue, or throat*
- *Itchy mouth*
- *Dizziness or light-headedness (potentially fainting)*
- *Diarrhea, nausea, or vomiting*
- *Wheezing or trouble breathing*
- *Hives or rash*
- *Anaphylaxis (the most severe)*

Signs can manifest immediately or take up to 2 hours. If you believe your baby is having an allergic reaction, seek medical advice immediately. Clean their hands and face and move them away from the food. Monitor your baby for swelling or lethargy.

Anaphylaxis is the most severe reaction. Symptoms include trouble breathing via constricted airways and tightening of the throat, rapid pulse, lethargy or loss in consciousness, or shock from a drop in blood pressure. If you suspect anaphylaxis, call an ambulance immediately.

How Much Should You Feed Your Baby?

The key is to start slow and follow your baby's cues. For the first month, start with one meal day, then increase to two meals a day. By nine months, aim for 3 meals a day.

12.3 STARTING WITH PUREES

When you decide it's time to introduce solids, you can start with purees and spoon-feed your baby. Make sure the purees are smooth in consistency, avoiding lumps or chunks. Allow your baby to practice eating from a spoon and encourage them to stop when they feel full.

Feel free to introduce a wide variety of food from the start, like meats, fruits, vegetables, beans, lentils, or yogurt. Make a large batch and then freeze some so you're not always cooking and blending.

Whenever possible, try to give your baby organic foods. When organic isn't an option, The Environmental Working Group announces an annual list specifying the 'clean fifteen' and 'dirty dozen,' specifying which fruits and vegetables contain the most and least pesticides. The Environmental Working Group is a nonprofit, nonpartisan organization working to protect our environmental health by changing industry standards so everyone can live their healthiest life.

Wash all produce by soaking it for 5 minutes with white or apple cider vinegar.

Remember, it's a gradual process. If your baby seems hesitant about new food, don't be discouraged because it often takes 8 to 10 tries or even more for them to develop a taste for it.

12.4 BABY-LED WEANING

As you embark on the journey of introducing solid foods to your precious one, a growing trend known as baby-led weaning is catching attention. It's not just about spoon-feeding purees; it's about empowering your baby to take control of their food choices right from the beginning.

Understanding Baby-Led Weaning

Baby-led weaning, a method gaining popularity in the U.K. and making its way to the U.S., involves offering age-appropriate finger foods instead of the traditional approach with purees. It centers around letting your baby explore and feed themselves wholesome foods. This approach becomes viable around 6 months when babies can start self-feeding.

Baby-weaning was the approach I took with my son. It's not the right approach for everyone, but it felt right for me. My reasons were:

- *Fostering Independence:* My baby learned to feed himself, as well as choose what and how much to eat. Babies given this control are said to be less picky eaters as toddlers.
- *Oral Skills:* Eating a variety of food consistencies and textures enables your baby to learn how to move their tongue, improve jaw strength and practice swallowing.

If you choose this route, I highly recommend getting a book or course dedicated entirely to this topic. I enjoyed the book *Baby Lead Weaning* by Gill Rapley and Tracey Murkett.

Advantages of Baby-Led Weaning

- *Texture Variety:* Encourages familiarity with diverse textures and flavors, potentially reducing the risk of future food allergies.
- *Obesity Prevention:* Allows babies to self-regulate food intake, possibly reducing the likelihood of developing obesity compared to traditional spoon-feeding.
- *Motor Skill Development:* Fosters fine motor skills by handling finger foods.

Challenges

- *Messiness:* Baby-led weaning can be messy, especially during the learning phase of handling foods.
- *Iron Intake:* Paying attention to iron intake is essential, especially for breastfed babies who may require supplements when introducing solids.

How to Initiate Baby-Led Weaning

- *Continue Breastfeeding or Bottle-Feeding:* Maintain regular nursing or bottle-feeding schedules as they remain crucial sources of nutrition.
- *Soft Textures:* Start with foods that are soft enough for easy gumming or chewing. Avoid introducing hard or crunchy options initially.
- *Age-Appropriate Preparation:* Tailor the way you cut food based on your child's age and development, progressing from strips to bite-sized pieces.

- *Share Meals Together:* Offer your baby the same food that you're eating, assuming it's given in the correct form. This also allows your baby to observe and mimic your eating habits.

Safety Tips

- *Avoid Choking Hazards:* Steer clear of foods like nuts, whole grapes, raw carrots, popcorn, fish with bones, raw apples, cherry tomatoes, and hot dogs to minimize the risk of choking. Meat should only be offered if prepared properly and softly cooked.
- *Supervise Eating:* Always keep a watchful eye on your baby during meals to ensure their safety.
- *Maintain Upright Posture:* Ensure your baby sits upright in a highchair while eating to reduce the risk of choking.
- *Monitor Allergic Reactions:* While introducing various foods, remain vigilant for any signs of allergies. Seek advice from your pediatrician regarding the introduction of common allergens.

Best Foods for Baby-Led Weaning

Explore soft fruits, vegetables, proteins, whole grains, and dairy. Steer clear of adding extra salt, sugar, or artificial sweeteners.

The texture should be soft enough that if you pinch it with your fingers, it would flatten easily. A common rule is to have the food be the width and length of your finger.

Think of it as food sticks, such as carrots, sweet potatoes, broccoli, or pumpkin. You can offer them smaller pieces once your baby has developed their pincer grasp.

Another great resource is the 'Solid Starts' app. It details what foods are recommended based on your baby's age and how to serve them.

This journey is as unique as your little one. Enjoy the messy yet joyful exploration of flavors together!

12.5 FIRST FOODS TO TRY

When choosing your baby's first foods, it's like setting off on a culinary adventure while keeping those essential nutritional needs in mind. Here's a quick checklist of nutrients to consider:

- Iron
- Zinc
- Healthy fats
- Calcium
- Choline
- Selenium
- Vitamin D

Now, let's explore some great initial food options for your little one!

Avocado

Loaded with vitamin B6, folate, vitamin E, potassium, and vitamin C, avocado serves as a nutrient-dense choice for your baby's brain development, thanks to its unsaturated fats.

Banana

A tasty source of carbohydrates, B vitamins, vitamin C, potassium, magnesium, and manganese, bananas offer energy, support immune function, and contribute to bone health.

Beef Liver

Often overlooked but rich in choline, vitamin A, iron, zinc, and more, beef liver is essential for cognitive development, eye health, and immune function.

Bell Pepper

Packed with provitamin A beta-carotene, vitamin C, vitamin E, and vitamin B6, bell peppers promote eye health, support the immune system, and aid in brain development.

Broccoli

An excellent source of vitamin C, vitamin K, folate, manganese, and magnesium, broccoli supports immune health, growth, and bone development.

Butternut Squash

Rich in vitamin C, beta-carotene, manganese, magnesium, and calcium, butternut squash boosts the immune system and contributes to eye health.

Chicken Liver

A powerhouse for blood health, immune function, and brain development, chicken liver is rich in iron, zinc, copper, choline, and vitamin A.

Chickpeas

High in fiber, folate, iron, manganese, and zinc, chickpeas are excellent for the immune system, bones, and red blood cells.

Eggs

Essential for eye and brain development, eggs are a nutrient-rich food high in protein, vitamin D, iron, choline, selenium, lutein, zeaxanthin, omega-3 fatty acids, folate, and B Vitamins. Their protein content contains all nine essential amino acids, which support the entire body.

Green Peas

Packed with B vitamins, vitamin C, vitamin K, manganese, phosphorus, iron, magnesium, and zinc, green peas contribute to overall health.

Lentils

As a plant-based protein, lentils offer fiber, iron, manganese, phosphorus, zinc, magnesium, and copper, supporting growth and development.

Mango

Rich in vitamin C, beta-carotene, vitamin B6, and vitamin E, mango promotes eye and immune health, as well as brain development.

Millet

Often overlooked but high in B vitamins, iron, magnesium, manganese, phosphorus, and zinc, millet aids in metabolism and energy production.

Oats

Providing energy and regulating blood sugars, oats are high in carbohydrates, fiber, magnesium, phosphorus, manganese, selenium, thiamine, pantothenic acid, and folate.

Peanut Butter

A brain and immune system booster, peanut butter is a healthy fat rich in phosphorus, copper, magnesium, manganese, zinc, vitamin E, and B vitamins.

12.6 FOODS TO AVOID WITHIN THE FIRST YEAR

There's a lot to consider when it comes to your baby's first year and food choices. Here's a brief guide to foods you might want to avoid:

Hard Foods: Steer clear of whole nuts, seeds, raw carrots, and similar hard foods for the first 3 years to minimize choking risks. Nut pastes are safe after 6 months.

Milk: Avoid fresh, unmodified milk from non-human sources (like cows, goats, and sheep) as the main drink before 12 months. Instead, go for full-cream cow's milk products after six months but not as the primary beverage.

Plant-based Milk: Plant-based milk like soy, rice, and oat aren't suitable for infants. Consider calcium-fortified varieties after 12 months under professional supervision.

Honey: Refrain from giving honey to babies under 12 months due to the risk of botulism. Never coat pacifiers or nipples with honey.

Sweeteners: Say no to sugar, honey, and other sweeteners in the first year. They don't contribute to nutrition and can lead to tooth decay.

Salt: Avoid adding salt to infant foods in their first year, as their organs can't handle excess salt. Skip salty foods to prevent developing a taste for them.

Low-fat Products: Children under 2 need the energy from full-fat products; low-fat versions aren't recommended.

Non-milk Beverages: Stick to breast milk or formula as the main drink for the first 12 months. Sterilized water is okay from around 6 months.

Fruit Juice: Say no to fruit juice for infants; it offers no nutritional benefits over whole fruit and can harm dental health.

Caffeinated and Sugary Drinks: Tea isn't suitable for infants, and coffee or caffeinated drinks should be avoided.

Raw and Unpasteurized: Be cautious with raw eggs, unpasteurized milk, fermented meat, undercooked meat, poultry, fish, shellfish, deli food, and leftovers to prevent contamination and food poisoning.

Remember, breastfeeding is recommended alongside solid foods or, if not, opt for infant formula since it's the primary source of nutrition for the first 12 months.

Remember, this is your unique journey, so take it one spoonful at a time! I highly recommend the book Milk to Meals by Luka McCabe and Carley Mendes for more details on baby eating guides.

———————

And that's the end of it, my fellow moms! The last chapter tackled one of the most daunting yet natural moments of your baby's growth: introducing solid foods! From the best foods to the worst ones, I have lent you my knowledge of getting your baby started on eating their first foods.

With this, we reached the end of this book's journey! But don't worry because this is the start of your own journey with your little one. And trust me when I say this, it will be one hell of a ride, which is why this book, and my tips and knowledge are here for you to lean on!

"Money can't buy happiness, but giving it away can."

— *FREDDIE MERCURY*

I have a question for you.

Would you help someone you've never met, even if you never got credit for it?

Who is this person you ask? They are like you. Or, at least, like you used to be. Less experienced, wanting to make a difference, and needing help, but unsure where to look.

Now you have everything you need to master being a first-time mom; it's time to pass on your newfound knowledge and show other readers where they can find the same help.

Simply by leaving your honest opinion of this book on Amazon, you'll show other new moms where they can find the information they're looking for and pass their passion for giving themselves and their babies the best care possible during this life-changing time.

Thank you for your help. First-Time Mom Made Simple is kept alive when we pass on our knowledge – and you're helping me do just that!

Simply scan the QR code below to leave your review:

Thank you for taking the time to leave your review and for joining me on this magnificent journey together!

Good luck!

- Andrea Mitchell

CONCLUSION

As we reach the culmination of this remarkable journey, my heart swells with appreciation for the strength and perseverance you've exhibited throughout the pages of this guide. From the anticipation of your birthing plan to the triumphs and trials of the initial year, we've navigated the unpredictable waters of motherhood side by side.

As you gear up for the next six months, armed with newfound insights and a toolbox of invaluable suggestions, remember that adaptability and self-kindness will serve as your strongest companions. The path ahead might not always align with expectations, and that's perfectly fine. Embrace spontaneity, celebrate the small wins, and be gentle with yourself when faced with challenges.

In the coming months, you'll witness your little one evolving into their unique self, achieving milestones that will fill your heart with delight and awe. As you enter this phase, take pleasure in every bonding moment, each giggle, and every tiny victory.

Preparing for the next six months goes beyond anticipating your baby's needs; it involves recognizing the evolving requirements of your own well-being. Nurture your physical recovery, attend to your emotional health, and find comfort in the support networks surrounding you. Motherhood is an ongoing growth journey for you and your baby.

In these final pages, permit me to offer a few closing thoughts and encouragement. Trust your instincts; you understand your baby better than anyone else. Rely on your support system; let them share in your successes and be there to lift you during challenging days. Embrace the rhythm of motherhood with an open heart and remember that you're never alone on this journey.

I commend you for the sleepless nights, the laughter, the tears, and the countless moments of boundless love. You are embarking on a transformative adventure that will shape your baby's future and weave the extraordinary tapestry of your own life.

As you conclude my book and step into the next stage of motherhood, may you do so with assurance, grace, and an abundance of love!

REFERENCES

The Art Of Swaddling: How To Safely Swaddle Your Newborn. (2022, May 23). Mothercare. Retrieved October 18, 2023, from https://www.mothercare.com. sg/blog/the-art-of-swaddling-how-to-safely-swaddle-your-newborn

Attygalla, T. (2022, April 5). HOW TO SET UP BABY'S NURSERY + NURSERY SET UP CHECKLIST. Nursery Design Studio. Retrieved October 17, 2023, from https://www.nurserydesignstudio.com/2022/04/05/how-to-set-up-babys-nursery-nursery-set-up-checklist/

Baby bath time essentials — The Organized Mom Life. (n.d.). The Organized Mom Life. Retrieved November 8, 2023, from https://theorganizedmomlife.com/ baby-bath-time-essentials/

Baby Crying | Crying Checklist For Parents. (n.d.). Kidspot NZ. Retrieved October 28, 2023, from https://kidspot.co.nz/baby/crying-checklist/

Barker, N. (2023, February 20). SETTLE DOWN! Our best settling techniques for babies. Little Ones. Retrieved October 25, 2023, from https://www.littleones. co/blog/settle-down-our-best-settling-techniques-for-babies

Cassey, N. (2017, November 1). 3 Step Swaddle Transition Plan - When to stop swaddling? Bubbaroo. Retrieved October 26, 2023, from https://www.bubba roo.com.au/blog/transitioning-baby-out-of-swaddling/

Colic and crying - self-care. (2023, July 1). MedlinePlus. Retrieved October 28, 2023, from https://medlineplus.gov/ency/patientinstructions/000753.htm

The Diapering Essentials Checklist: Unraveling the Must-Haves. (2023, August 12). By a mom, for moms | Practical Little Life. Retrieved November 8, 2023, from https://practicallittlelife.com/diapering-essentials/

Does Your Baby Have Gas? Signs of Infant Gas and How to Treat It. (2023, June 29). Parents. Retrieved October 28, 2023, from https://www.parents.com/baby/ care/gas/signs-newborn-has-gas/

Duchene, D. (2016, November 1). 6 Ways to Get Back in Shape Post-Baby – Johnson Fitness and Wellness. Johnson Fitness. Retrieved November 11, 2023, from https://www.johnsonfitness.com/blog/6-ways-get-back-shape-post-baby/

Miranda Castro Homeopathy. (n.d.). An Emotional Roller Coaster: Recovery After Birth. Miranda Castro's. Retrieved October 17, 2023, from https://mirandacas tro.com/emotional-recovery-after-birth/

Centuary Mattress. (n.d.). Finding a Balance Between Work and Life as a New

Mom. Retrieved November 13, 2023, from https://www.centuaryindia.com/blog/finding-a-balance-between-work-and-life-as-a-new-mom/

Kinsa. (n.d.). First Day Checklist: 7 Things You Need When Bringing Baby Home. Retrieved October 16, 2023, from https://home.kinsahealth.com/post/7-things-you-need-when-bringing-baby-home

Gavin, M. L. (n.d.). When Can My Baby Start Eating Solid Foods? (for Parents) - Nemours KidsHealth. Kids Health. Retrieved November 14, 2023, from https://kidshealth.org/en/parents/solid-foods.html

Gill, K. (2019, July 31). Baby Wearing: Benefits, Safety Tips, How-To, Carrier Types & More. Healthline. Retrieved November 9, 2023, from https://www.healthline.com/health/parenting/baby-wearing#how-to

Gill, K., & Bjarnadottir, A. (2020, April 14). The 4-Month Sleep Regression: What to Do. Healthline. Retrieved October 28, 2023, from https://www.healthline.com/health/parenting/4-month-sleep-regression#tips-for-managing-sleep-regression

Gordon, S. (2023, January 19). 9 Steps to Planning Your Maternity Leave. Verywell Family. Retrieved November 13, 2023, from https://www.verywellfamily.com/steps-to-planning-maternity-leave-4174656

Guide, S. (n.d.). Feeding your baby with formula | Pregnancy Birth and Baby. Pregnancy, Birth and Baby. Retrieved October 27, 2023, from https://www.pregnancybirthbaby.org.au/feeding-your-baby-with-formula

Parents. (2023, July 17). How to Deal With Sleep Deprivation After Baby. Retrieved October 17, 2023, from https://www.parents.com/baby/new-parent/sleep-deprivation/how-to-get-sleep/

Happiest Baby. (n.d.). How to Sleep Train Your Baby. Retrieved October 26, 2023, from https://www.happiestbaby.com/blogs/baby/sleep-training

Kim, H. (n.d.). 25 Best First Foods for Baby. Kids Eat in Color. Retrieved November 14, 2023, from https://kidseatincolor.com/best-first-foods-for-baby/

Kotlen, M. (2021, July 16). Breastfeeding Basics - Everything You Need to Know. Verywell Family. Retrieved October 27, 2023, from https://www.verywellfamily.com/breastfeeding-basics-431679

Kurtz, D. (2015, November 9). 4 Ways to Ease a Teething Baby. Intermountain Healthcare. Retrieved October 28, 2023, from https://intermountainhealthcare.org/blogs/teething-and-babies

Pregnancy, Birth and Baby. (n.d.). Learning to walk. Retrieved November 12, 2023, from https://www.pregnancybirthbaby.org.au/learning-to-walk

Lee, J. (2023, March 10). How to Prepare for Maternity Leave - Workest. Zenefits. Retrieved November 13, 2023, from https://www.zenefits.com/workest/how-to-prepare-for-maternity-leave/

Seattle Children's. (2022, December 30). Newborn Illness - How to Recognize.

Retrieved November 9, 2023, from https://www.seattlechildrens.org/condi tions/a-z/newborn-illness-how-to-recognize/

FamilyDoctor.org. (2017, September 7). Newborn Sleep Routines. Retrieved October 26, 2023, from https://familydoctor.org/newborn-sleep-routines/

NowPsych. (2023, November 6). 25 Best Toys for Baby Development (According to a Child Psychiatrist) - Updated for 2023. Retrieved November 12, 2023, from https://nowpsych.com/best-toys-for-baby-development/

Allina Health. (n.d.). Postpartum Emotions | Postpartum Depression. Retrieved November 11, 2023, from https://www.allinahealth.org/health-conditions- and-treatments/health-library/patient-education/beginnings/your-recovery- at-home/your-emotions

FamilyDoctor.org. (2017, January 26). Postpartum Recovery - Recovering From Delivery. Retrieved November 11, 2023, from https://familydoctor.org/recover ing-from-delivery/

Boober. (n.d.). Preparing for Postpartum. Retrieved October 18, 2023, from https:// getboober.com/preparing-for-postpartum/

Breastmilk Counts. (n.d.). Pump and Store | Breastfeeding Basics. Retrieved October 27, 2023, from https://www.breastmilkcounts.com/breastfeeding- basics/pump-and-store/

Rickards, S. (n.d.). Foods To Avoid In the First Year. Newborn Baby. Retrieved November 14, 2023, from https://newbornbaby.com.au/newborn-overview/ baby-feeding/foods-to-avoid-in-the-first-year/

Nationwide Children's Hospital. (n.d.). Safe Sleep Practices for Babies. Retrieved October 26, 2023, from https://www.nationwidechildrens.org/family- resources-education/health-wellness-and-safety-resources/helping-hands/ safe-sleep-practices-for-babies

Schweet, C. (2023, April 5). Complete Guide: How to Dress Your Baby by Temperature. Hello Postpartum. Retrieved October 25, 2023, from https:// hellopostpartum.com/how-to-dress-baby-by-temperature/

Pampers. (2021, April 5). Skin-to-Skin Contact: The Benefits of Kangaroo Care. Retrieved November 9, 2023, from https://www.pampers.com/en-us/preg nancy/giving-birth/article/skin-to-skin-contact

What to Expect. (2021, June 9). The 4th Trimester of Pregnancy: What It Is, Tips for Coping. Retrieved October 16, 2023, from https://www.whattoexpect.com/ first-year/postpartum/what-doctors-wish-moms-knew-fourth-trimester/

What to Expect. (2022, November 9). Baby-Led Weaning (BLW): Best Foods for Baby-Led Weaning & How to Start. Retrieved November 14, 2023, from https://www.whattoexpect.com/first-year/feeding-baby/baby-led-weaning/

WebMD. (2023, July 11). Why the Fourth Trimester Is So Important for Mom and

Baby. Retrieved October 16, 2023, from https://www.webmd.com/baby/what-is-the-fourth-trimester

Restful Parenting. (2023, January 10). Transitioning baby from arms to bassinet/crib. Retrieved October 26, 2023, from https://restfulparenting.com/sleep-tips/transitioning-baby-from-arms-to-crib

BabyCenter. (2022, March 10). How much interaction and playtime newborns and babies need. Retrieved November 9, 2023, from https://www.babycenter.com/baby/baby-development/how-much-do-i-have-to-play-and-interact-with-my-baby-do-babi_6882

WebMD. (2022, August 9). Baby Vaccine Schedule: What Shots Baby Needs and When. Retrieved November 9, 2023, from https://www.webmd.com/parenting/baby/vaccination-schedule-what-to-expect

BabyCentre. (n.d.). Understanding your newborn. Retrieved November 12, 2023, from https://www.babycentre.co.uk/a1047903/understanding-your-newborn

Cleveland Clinic. (n.d.). Colostrum & the Stages of Breast Milk. Retrieved from https://my.clevelandclinic.org/health/body/22434-colostrum

KidsHealth. (n.d.). Your Newborn's Growth. Retrieved from https://kidshealth.org/en/parents/grownewborn.html.

Tresillian. (n.d.). Respond to Babies Cries: 0-3 months. Retrieved from https://www.tresillian.org.au/advice-tips/crying/0-3-months/

Pregnancy, Birth, and Baby. (n.d.). What Is the Fourth Trimester? Retrieved from https://www.pregnancybirthbaby.org.au/what-is-the-fourth-trimester.

Red Nose. (n.d.). How to Dress Baby for Sleep. Retrieved from https://rednose.org.au/article/how-to-dress-baby-for-sleep

Lancaster General Health. (n.d.). Understanding and Navigating Sleep Regressions. Retrieved from https://www.lancastergeneralhealth.org/health-hub-home/motherhood/the-first-year/understanding-and-navigating-sleep-regressions

Happiest Baby. (n.d.). The Importance of Sleep. Retrieved from https://www.happiestbaby.com/blogs/baby/importance-of-sleep

Parents. (n.d.). 7 Things to Do With Your Placenta Besides Leaving It at the Hospital. Retrieved from https://www.parents.com/pregnancy/giving-birth/labor-and-delivery/7-things-to-do-with-your-placenta-besides-leaving-it-at/

Healthline. (n.d.). Delayed Cord Clamping: How It Works. Retrieved from https://www.healthline.com/health/pregnancy/delayed-cord-clamping#how-it-works

Raising Children Network. (n.d.). Understanding Sleep: Tired Signs. Retrieved from https://raisingchildren.net.au/babies/sleep/understanding-sleep/tired-signs?gclid=Cj0KCQiA4NWrBhD-ARIsAFCKwWtnAZASy5Qsih4Y74F5gRI6MjFt3Alz9rb7KwY1hdySIm5V8FpRp1saAqVIEALw_wcB

Donate Life. (n.d.). Birth Tissue Donation. Retrieved from https://donatelife.net/donation/organs/birth-tissue/

Healthline. (n.d.). How to Bottle Feed a Baby: Positions, Tips, and More. Retrieved from https://www.healthline.com/health/baby/how-to-bottle-feed-a-baby#positions

Twiniversity. (n.d.). The Dos and Don'ts of Bottle Feeding Your Baby. Retrieved from https://www.twiniversity.com/dos-donts-bottle-feeding/

Fed Is Best Foundation. (2022, May 26). Why It's Time to Stop Teaching Parents Paced Bottle Feeding and Teach Responsive Feeding as Recommended by the AAP. Retrieved from https://fedisbest.org/2022/05/why-its-time-to-stop-teaching-parents-paced-bottle-feeding-and-teach-responsive-feeding-as-recommended-by-the-aap/

Parents. (n.d.). Baby Feeding Chart: How Much and When to Feed Infants in the First Year. Retrieved from https://www.parents.com/baby/feeding/baby-feeding-chart-how-much-and-when-to-feed-infants-the-first-year/

San Diego Breastfeeding Center. (2014, December 9). On-Demand vs. Scheduled Feeding: Which Is Best for Baby? Retrieved from https://www.sdbfc.com/blog/2014/12/9/on-demand-vs-scheduled-feeding-which-is-best-for-baby

The Bump. (n.d.). Building a Breast Milk Stash Before You Go Back to Work. Retrieved from https://www.thebump.com/a/building-a-breast-milk-stash-before-you-go-back-to-work

Harvard Health Publishing. (2017, October 31). Why Parents Should Save Their Baby's Cord Blood — and Give It Away. Retrieved from https://www.health.harvard.edu/blog/why-parents-should-save-their-babys-cord-blood-and-give-it-away-201710312518

Royal Children's Hospital Melbourne. (n.d.). Fact Sheet: Fever in Children. Retrieved from https://www.rch.org.au/kidsinfo/fact_sheets/fever_in_children/

Raising Children Network. (n.d.). Newborns: Umbilical Care. Retrieved from https://raisingchildren.net.au/newborns/health-daily-care/hygiene-keeping-clean/umbilical-care

Pregnancy, Birth and Baby. (n.d.). Understanding Your Newborn. Retrieved from https://www.pregnancybirthbaby.org.au/umbilical-care

Raising Children Network. (n.d.). Talking With Babies and Toddlers. Retrieved from https://raisingchildren.net.au/babies/connecting-communicating/communicating/talking-with-babies-toddlers

Nurtured Noggins. (n.d.). 20 Ways to Play With a 0-3 Month Old. Retrieved from https://nurturednoggins.com/20-ways-to-play-with-a-0-3-month-old/

Nurtured Noggins. (n.d.). 12 Activities for 3-6 Month Olds. Retrieved from https://nurturednoggins.com/12-activities-for-3-6-month-old/

Raising Children Network. (n.d.). Baby Development. Retrieved from https://raisingchildren.net.au/newborns/development/understanding-development/baby-development

Pregnancy, Birth, and Baby. (n.d.). Baby Development. Retrieved from https://www.pregnancybirthbaby.org.au/baby-development

Palumbo, J. (2023, April 21). 5 Proven Tips for Balancing Your Career and Motherhood. Forbes. Retrieved from https://www.forbes.com/sites/jenniferpalumbo/2023/04/21/5-proven-tips-for-balancing-your-career-and-motherhood/?sh=632e0d8d5541

Loveliemoreno. (2023, December 28). Encouraging words: Quotes to uplift new moms | Blissbies. *Blissbies.* https://blissbies.com/blog/quotes-words-of-encouragement-for-new-mothers/

McCable, L & Mendes, C (2020) Milk to Meals, Publication Design and Illustration.

Viacord (2023). How cord blood is used today. Retrieved from https://www.viacord.com/treatments-and-research/how-cord-blood-is-used-today/

Australian Breastfeeding Association. (2022, April). Feeding cues. Australian Breastfeeding Association. https://www.breastfeeding.asn.au/resources/feeding-cues

Nest Collaborative. (n.d.). Everything You Need to Know About Breast Milk Production and Supply. Retrieved January 13, 2024, from https://nestcollaborative.com/blog/everything-you-need-to-know-about-breast-milk-production-supply/

Nationwide Children's Hospital. (n.d.). Babies' Warning Signs. Retrieved January 13, 2024, from https://www.nationwidechildrens.org/family-resources-education/family-resources-library/babies-warning-signs

Solid Starts. (n.d.). What is Baby-Led Weaning? Benefits of BLW. Retrieved January 14, 2024, from https://solidstarts.com/baby-led-weaning/

Hackensack Meridian Health. (2023, March 2). What happens to your hormones after birth? HealthU. https://www.hackensackmeridianhealth.org/en/healthu/2023/03/02/what-happens-to-your-hormones-after-birth

Patel, A. (2015). A newly found relationship between heat and sudden infant death syndrome. *Inquiro: Journal of Undergraduate Research, 9.* Retrieved from https://www.uab.edu/inquiro/issues/past-issues/volume-9/a-newly-found-relationship-between-heat-and-sudden-infant-death-syndrome

Gontcharova, N. (2023, August 3). How the concept of 'matrescence' can help you navigate parenthood. *The Bump.* Retrieved from https://www.thebump.com/a/matrescence

Happiest Baby Staff. (n.d.). Is it safe for my baby to sleep in a car seat? *Happiest Baby.* Retrieved from https://www.happiestbaby.com/blogs/baby/baby-sleeping-in-car-seat-at-night

Centers for Disease Control and Prevention. (2023). Drowning prevention. *CDC*

Vital Signs. Retrieved from https://www.cdc.gov/vitalsigns/drowning/index.html

Karp, H. (n.d.). *How much do babies sleep? A sleep schedule for your baby's first year.* Happiest Baby. Retrieved August 10, 2024, from https://www.happiestbaby.com/blogs/baby/first-year-sleep-schedule

Kim, H., & Filemon, J. (2022, October). *The benefits of eggs for babies + how to serve them safely.* Kids Eat in Color. https://kidseatincolor.com/eggs-for-babies/

www.ingramcontent.com/pod-product-compliance
Lightning Source LLC
Chambersburg PA
CBHW060804120626
46557CB00001B/88